QIGONG
TEACHINGS
OF A
TAOIST
IMMORTAL

OTHER BOOKS BY STUART OLSON

T'ai Chi According to the I Ching

Tai Chi for Kids

Tao of No Stress

QIGONG TEACHINGS
OF A
TAOIST IMMORTAL

THE EIGHT ESSENTIAL EXERCISES
OF MASTER LI CHING-YUN

STUART ALVE OLSON

Healing Arts Press
Rochester, Vermont

Healing Arts Press
One Park Street
Rochester, Vermont 05767
www.InnerTraditions.com

Healing Arts Press is a division of Inner Traditions International

*Note to the reader: This book is intended as an informational guide. The remedies, approaches,
and techniques described herein are meant to supplement, and not to be a substitute for, professional medical
care or treatment. They should not be used to treat a serious ailment without prior
consultation with a qualified health care professional.*

Library of Congress Cataloging-in-Publication Data

Olson, Stuart Alve.
    Qigong teachings of a taoist immortal : the eight essential exercises
of master li ching-yun / Stuart Alve Olson.
        p. cm.
Includes bibliographical references and index.
    ISBN 978-089281945-4
    1. Qi gong. I. Title: Eight essential exercises of master li ching-yun. II. Title.
    RA781.8 .O46 2002
    613.7'1—dc21

                                                        2001006070

Printed and bound in the United States

11 10

Text design and layout by Rachel Goldenberg

This book was typeset in Legacy with Oxalis as the display typeface

To my son, Lee Jin.
A golden benefit you really are.

CONTENTS

PART 3

THE LESSER HEAVENLY CIRCUIT—THE SPIRITUAL PRACTICE

ACKNOWLEDGMENTS

For providing me with the finest instruction and patience, I must thank Ch'an master Hsuan Hua, t'ai chi ch'uan master Tung-tsai Liang, Zen master Dainan Katagiri, dharma master Chen Yi, and master healer Oei Kong-wei.

Special thanks to Patrick Gross for all his early editing and formatting of the text, and to Richard Peterson for the incredible cover photo collage and the photos that illustrate each exercise.

*"People's natures are basically the same;
it is their practices which set them far apart."*
— **Confucius**

INTRODUCTION

The purpose and hope for this work, beyond the sharing of these marvelous ancient Taoist teachings with the public, is that its contents will help clarify and add a proper depth of meaning to the many oversimplified explanations given in so many of the popular Taoist and qigong books available in English today. I hope that it will also make clear the many overly mystified explanations that predominate in these popular writings as well.

The Taoist Canon (Tao tsang) consists of some 1,600-plus volumes, of which 75 percent deal primarily with the so-called arts of nourishing life (yang sheng shu), of which qigong is a part. It would be unreasonable to assume that any one book could possibly elucidate completely the teachings of Taoism; this work represents but a small fraction of the ancient wisdom. But what this book does do, if I have been successful, is provide a useful explanation of Taoist restorative and healing arts and comprehensive instructions on the most effective series of qigong longevity exercises developed by the Taoists, called the Eight Brocades and the Lesser Heavenly Circuit.

What makes this work unique, however, is not just its instructions on these Taoist practices but its commentaries on the exercises by the highly respected master Li Ching-yun. Li Ching-yun is one of the most famous Taoist masters of this century. He reportedly practiced these exercises for more than one hundred years, and historical documents show that he was 256 years old at the time of his death in the early 1930s. His explanations, endorsements, and longevity attest to and validate the Eight Brocades as the culmination of Taoist health and qigong practices.

Although this book deals primarily with Taoist practices, it reveals so much more about Taoism in general than could ever be learned from just studying Taoist historical and philosophical works. Practice and philosophy go hand in hand, being just two sides of the same coin. Whether you choose to practice any of the exercises in this book, your understanding of Taoism will be greatly increased by just reading it.

The book has been organized to accommodate both the advanced and the beginning student. The text relies upon several works that I have translated from the Chinese as well as upon my own practice of qigong. The primary translation comes from a stone rubbing of the original Eight Brocades text by Kao Lin of the early Ching dynasty (circa seventeenth century A.D.). (Note: The Eight Brocades text was reproduced for the stone rubbing; the date that it was first drafted is unknown.) Also included are extensive translated passages from General Yang Shen's biography of the immortal Li Ching-yun, published in Wan Hsien, China, in 1936. Where I deemed them informative, I have translated small passages from other works as well, but it is not necessary to list them all here.

Basically the reader will encounter three separate voices in the material: that of the Kao Lin text, that of Li Ching-yun, and of course, my own voice, usually designated "Author's Comments." The translated voices were originally presented in separate sections, with my comments included as footnotes, but that arrangement resulted in a lot of repetition. Ultimately, I found it simpler for readers to follow the material if everything was contained in one running text.

The book provides a background explanation of the Eight Brocades, the how-to aspects of the form, and supplementary techniques to further develop your practice. To learn the exercises, it is important to read the entire book first, then begin performing the exercises according to the instructions provided.

Whether you are just starting out in learning about Taoism or are already engaged in Taoist practices, you will find many new and wonderful insights in the contents of this work, as many portions are appearing in English for the first time.

PART 1

THE DEVELOPMENT OF QIGONG

TAOIST LONGEVITY PRACTICES AND THE THREE TREASURES

八段錦 Taoist Longevity Practices

Throughout history, Taoists have propagated the development and restoration of the human body, breath, and spirit. They call these the Three Treasures (san pao): ching, qi, and shen, corresponding in simplest terms to body, breath, and spirit. The human body results from the culmination of sexual forces, or ching, is animated by the vital force of qi, and made conscious through the activation of shen. By preserving the Three Treasures, Taoists believe that people can achieve optimal health and longevity and also create within themselves the alchemical gate to immortality.

The Arts of Nourishing Life

Three practices dominate the Taoist quest for health, longevity, and immortality. The first is the ingestion of herbal medicines (fu erh) and the purification dietary regimes. The second is the performance of physical and respiratory exercises (t'u na) to gain breath control and mobilize the qi. The third practice is the achievement of mental and physical tranquility through meditation (ching tso). If one or more of these three practices can be maintained in your daily life, you will at the very least restore your vitality and stamina (having youthfulness in old age). Depending on the depth and sincerity of your efforts, you could attain longevity (living to over one hundred years of age in good health) or actually discover the elixir of immortality.

Many Taoists consider longevity (shou) to mean the ability to experience youthfulness in old age and to live in good health to the end of one's days. Sickness prevents practitioners from putting all their effort toward immortality, and death ensures failure. The notion of living beyond one hundred years of age has always been considered a milepost of sorts, proving to everyone that your art and teaching have merit.

The term corresponding to immortality *(hsien)* literally means "man in the mountains." The idea is of a hermit seeking complete absorption into nature. Many schools of Taoism, however, do believe and propagate the idea of actual physical immortality. The most widely accepted meaning contends that when the practitioner dies, the mental and spiritual energies remain intact after death; in other words, the practitioner remains completely conscious during the death experience. In Taoist terms, the heavenly spirit (hun) remains, while the earthly spirit (p'o) is shed.

In order to preserve the Three Treasures and forge the elixir of immortality, Taoists developed physical and respiratory exercises that originally were placed under the general heading of arts of nourishing life. The entire basis for what is now popularly called qigong began with the simple experiment of healing with the breath, which in turn led to the discovery of qi energy itself.

Qi literally means "breath" and "vital energy." The term is one of the most extensively used in the Chinese language, and is applied to anything which incorporates the idea of energy, such as *t'ien qi,* meaning "heaven's breath" or more simply "weather." But for the purpose of this material the qi referred to is contained within the idea of the vital energy, which both sustains life and animates it. Qi to the Chinese mind is the very energy that allows us to be mobile and active. The main source of qi is in our breath, wherein we are constantly breathing in qi.

The qi is also contained within meridians (energy pathways) and cavities of the body. When we learn to fully stimulate and awaken this energy, our bodies take on a new and heightened sense of vitality and power. We can access our qi in much the same way that we can access the power of steam to run a steam engine. Actually, in the Chinese the character for *qi* refers to the steam coming off the pot of cooking rice.

Through the stimulation and accumulation of qi a person may not only acquire a new sense of physical and mental energy, but create the conditions of longevity as well. Hence, there are numerous practices under the heading of qigong. But the Eight Brocades is actually the earliest regime of qigong; all others styles or practices created since have basically borrowed from the methods of the Eight Brocades.

In order to fully mobilize the qi throughout the body, one must first accumulate it in what is called the *tan-t'ien* (Field of Elixir). This tan-t'ien is a point in the lower abdomen about three inches below the navel and one inch back into the body. This area, normally called a "qi cavity," is not real in the sense of being something substantial; it is a mentally produced area at which a person feels his or her center of being. When the qi is felt there, usually by sensations of heat and vibration, it is also possible to circulate it and feel it move physically up along the spine, over the head, and back down into the tan-t'ien again. It is this very mobilization of qi that every Taoist aspires to. When nine complete circulations can be accomplished in one sitting, what is called an "immortal fetus" is produced. This immortal fetus is one's spiritual body, or "qi body" as it is sometimes referred to. In brief, immortality is achieved.

Chuang-tzu

The Taoists are not alone in their theory of qi. Similar theories are seen in yoga practices (where qi is called *prana*) and in various other religions and philosophies as well. But all of these theories originate in the breath, which is why the term *qigong* itself means "skillful breathing."

Through simply breathing in deeply and then focusing the exhalation and visualizing the breath expelling through the location of the pain or affliction, the early Chinese discovered not only a great healing power but an internal energy as well. Later terms for the practice of these exercises included *t'u na* (literally to spit out and take in), *hsing qi* (moving the qi), *pi qi* (holding the qi), *tao yin* (leading and stimulating), *yun qi* (circulating the qi), *hsiao chou t'ien* (the Lesser Heavenly Circuit), and the "skillful breathing" that is now generically referred to as *qigong* (a more literal meaning would be "exercising the qi").

The terms *t'u na* and *tao yin* first appeared in chapter fifteen of *Chuang-tzu* (named after its author, who lived circa 369–286 B.C.), where it says:

Breathing in and out in various manners, spitting out the old and taking in the new, walking like a bear and stretching their necks like a bird to achieve longevity—this is what such practitioners of tao yin, cultivators of the body and all those searching for long life like Ancestor Peng, enjoy.

Tao in combination with qi means "guiding the breath," and yin used with qi means "to stimulate the breath." The premise of tao yin then is physical movement done in conjunction with the breath in order to mobilize the qi throughout the body. The meaning of this term goes far deeper, however, than this simple definition.

At Ma-wang-tui near Ch'ang-sha in Hunan Province, a large length of silk from the early Han dynasty (approximately 206 B.C. to 23 B.C.) was discovered in an unearthed tomb. Painted on this silk were forty-four figures clearly performing tao yin exercises, and so it was given the name Tao Yin Tu (tao yin chart). A series of the drawings were prefixed with the word yin, but here the meaning is to "induce a cure." So the early meaning of tao yin appears to have been "leading the breath to induce a cure."

In his discourses on *Chuang-tzu,* Li Yi, an early Han dynasty Taoist, describes tao as the process of "guiding the breath to make it harmonious" and yin as "leading the body to become soft." Soft carries many meanings,

Peng-tzu, an ancient immortal who reputedly lived during the Shang dynasty (1766 B.C. to 1154 B.C.). The Book of History* lists him as having lived over eight hundred years.

such as flexible, pliable, open, relaxed, sensitive, alert, and so on. It is through softness, the elimination of tension, that qi is able to freely move about the body through the meridians and collaterals, which is precisely what hsing qi refers to.

The earliest known appearance of hsing qi is on the handle of a staff unearthed in Shantung Province, dated circa 380 B.C. The inlaid jade inscriptions,

---

*The Book of History is a Confucian classic written by Ssu Ma-hsien during the Chou dynasty (1122 B.C. to 255 B.C.) that provides a record of famous personages of Chinese history from that period and preceding periods.

Emperor Huang Ti

in referring to the purpose and ensuing sensations of stopping the breath (pi qi), speak of the mobilization of breath, or hsing qi.

Hsing qi as a Taoist practice developed from the *Huang ti nei ching* (The Yellow Emperor's Classic of Internal Medicine), a medical book that appeared sometime during the third century B.C. but that presents itself as a set of teachings created for the Yellow Emperor (who ascended the throne in 2697 B.C.). In the chapter on "Plain Questions," we find the instructions for what Taoists came to call tortoise breathing (kuei hsi, literally "swallowing the breath"):

Breathe deeply seven times, each time stopping the breath qi extending the neck, and then swallowing the breath. It should be done as if one is swallowing something hard. Having done this seven times, move the tongue around and swallow the saliva that is produced several times.

About six hundred years later, Ko Hung, a fourth century A.D. Taoist alchemist adept and writer, reports that his uncle, Ko Hsuan, would sit at the bottom of a pond holding his breath for almost an entire day when the summer heat was too unbearable. This is an indication that Ko Hsuan was very adept at stopping the breath.

In many instances in his work *Pao-p'u-tzu,* Ko Hung advocates these types of breathing for the attainment of longevity and immortality.

Ko Hung

Abdominal Breathing

Ancient Taoists were great observers of life and its functions, especially of the process of continual dissipation and the rising of the breath during a person's life. When we are newly born, barring any problems created during the pregnancy, we are at our all-time best. Every day thereafter becomes a race toward death. We all start out in life with our breath very low in our abdomen, and our entire body breathes. As small sleeping babies, we breathed perfectly. Our bodies were warm and rosy colored, and our hands and feet received a strong, continuous supply of blood.

The problem is that as we get older we become conscious of the state of our health; as young children, contrarily, we are not conscious of it. In fact, we have no thoughts of good or bad health as children. As we grow older, we start to deal with anxiety, tension, responsibilities, sex, money, emotions, and so on—all of which cause our breath to rise. Our breath moves from the lower abdomen to the upper abdomen and into the lung area. Between the ages of thirty and fifty, most of us maintain our breathing in the solar plexus region. In our sixties and seventies, it rises to the lung area. If we are fortunate enough to die a natural death, the qi departs from the body with one last gasp for air.

Men in their old age will, generally speaking, acquire a "bird's chest" from accumulated air in the front upper lung area. This is the nature of the yang in men. Because of this, men lose their central equilibrium in old age, stumbling and wobbling with a body that is top-heavy with air. Their center of balance lies in the upper front lung area, which causes a slight leaning up and back.

Women, on the other hand, can acquire the "willow back" in their senior years from accumulated air in the upper back of the lungs. This is the nature of yin in women. The weight of the air is attracted to the upper back lung region, causing the spine and head to bend forward as if they were carrying a great weight on their backs. Since these are general trends and not true in all cases, some men, depending on their nature (yang or yin), can acquire either the bird's chest or the willow back; and so too for women.

Although it might look similar, the willow back should not be confused with what the Taoists call the "tortoise back," which is the result of the proper internal application of mobilizing qi through the Lesser Heavenly Circuit. If people can manage to keep their breath low throughout their entire life, they will probably not suffer from the negative conditions of the bird's chest or the willow back.

Ancient Taoists, who observed this pattern of the breath rising during a person's life and the final exit out the mouth at death, concluded that if a person is to attain longevity and perfect health, then the first rule is to restore the breath to the lower abdomen, where infants breathe. Lao-tzu, in his classic the *Tao-te ching,* asks, "Can you attain the pliability of a child?" He also states that "the entire secret of self-cultivation lies in subtraction, not in addition." This means that we must reverse our thinking, habits, and ambitions in order to preserve our health. Almost everything concerning Taoism focuses itself on returning to a state of youthfulness. Don't confuse this idea, however, with the Western infatuation with looking young.

Lao-tzu

Taoists value an aged person who is still vital and young in mind far more than someone in his or her youth. The reason and wisdom that come with age are what is valued. A common phrase in all Taoist works is *chang sheng pu lao,* which in literal translation would be "living long with no aging." More correctly, it means "youthfulness in longevity."

Enjoying youthfulness in old age, and thus prolonging life itself, is the first goal of Taoism because it renders more time for the refinement of the elixir and the attainment of immortality. And to undergo the rigors of self-cultivation one cannot afford to be sick or to lack vitality. Taoism's main tenet of returning the breath to the lower abdomen where it was when we were children makes perfect sense whether you are searching for good health, longevity, or immortality.

THE THREE TREASURES

The Three Treasures in their most basic definitions represent the primal and accumulated energies of the body (ching), breath (qi), and mind (shen)—both in the physical connotations and in the spiritual sense. To understand these three energies, you must first know the important role played by "before heaven qi" (hsien t'ien qi) and "after heaven qi" (hou t'ien qi).

Before heaven qi is the quality and quantity, so to speak, of these three energies inherited from our ancestors and parents. After heaven qi is what we accumulate from our own efforts. So we might say that people who abuse their bodies their whole lives but live a long time have a lot of before heaven qi. Whereas people who are sickly in their youth have inherited very little. However, these same sickly people who engage in the arts of nourishing life practices can accumulate enough after heaven qi to live long, healthy lives.

In order to understand the meaning and function of the Three Treasures, it helps to first examine the actual Chinese characters for ching, qi, and shen and to know why the Taoists elected to incorporate them.

The character for ching is comprised of the main radical *mi*, which symbolizes uncooked rice. It also contains the radical *sheng*, which holds the meanings of life and birth. Lastly, the radical *tan* is employed, meaning the essence of life. The symbol for tan carries the idea of the hue of a plant just sprouting—the white, green, and yellow hues that first burst forth. This idea is equated with the essence of life itself and is thereby extended to that of elixir.

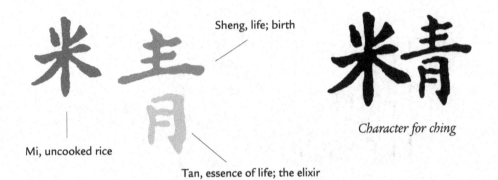

Sheng, life; birth

Mi, uncooked rice

Tan, essence of life; the elixir

Character for ching

The ideogram for qi depicts rice *(mi)* being cooked. Above the pot we see *yun,* which depicts the vapors coming off the top of the pot. The radical *chih* represents the pot in which the rice is cooked, or the abdomen in which the liquid (blood) is heated. The vapors coming off the pot are qi as an energy. They can also be viewed as clouds (earth's steam). Our breath serves not only as a process for sustaining life (as cooking is to eating) but as a catalyst for producing energy (as cooking produces steam). In representing qi as vapor or steam—which drives pistons in powerful engines—this ideogram clearly symbolizes the energy and power of qi.

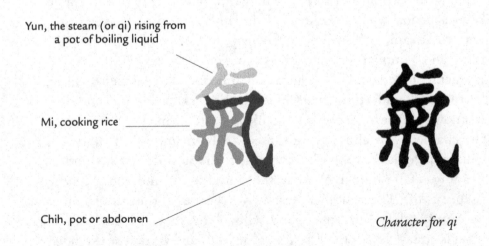

Yun, the steam (or qi) rising from a pot of boiling liquid

Mi, cooking rice

Chih, pot or abdomen

Character for qi

The character for *shen* is made up of *shih,* which means the origin or highest order of things. In brief, it depicts those things coming from heaven—the sun, moon, and stars. Next to it we see *t'ien,* which depicts a field, or paddy. The vertical line running through it symbolizes the connection of heaven and earth. The implied meaning here is the origin of things (shih) that connects people to heaven and earth and that is found in the fields from which sustenance is got. People can connect themselves to physical fields, human fields, and heavenly (spiritual) fields.

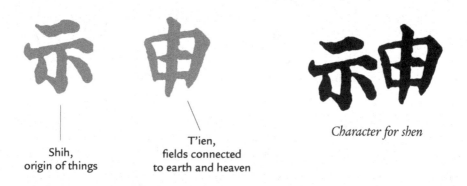

Shih,
origin of things

T'ien,
fields connected
to earth and heaven

Character for shen

In light of these three characters, the meaning of the term *tan t'ien* (referring to the lower abdominal region) can be grasped. *Tan* means elixir and, as stated, *t'ien* means field or paddy. It is within the very emptiness of our abdomen that tan t'ien exists. It is where we become spiritually pregnant and give birth to our spirit child—our restored youthfulness.

Tan t'ien is the spiritual equivalent of the fetus inside a woman's uterus, of raw rice being cooked in a pot, of ore being smelted inside a furnace, but most significantly, it is the place where ching and qi unite and create the spiritual embryo; it is the place where qi, our spiritual food, is cooked and where we refine raw essences into pure essences. The analogies are seemingly endless, but the idea is always the same: refinement of our natural life essences—ching, qi, and shen.

Ching

Taoists call the regenerative force in human beings ching, and they equate it with the body's physical strength and vitality. Ching is by definition sexual energy, sexual secretions, blood, food, and saliva. The arts of nourishing life methods sought to

Ching

restore ching to its condition in a person's childhood. Ching is the body's natural life energy and is acquired through nourishment and is dissipated through exertion, both physical and mental.

Ching can be thought of as containing three distinct physical aspects: 1) sexual secretions; 2) blood and the nutrients within it; and 3) flesh and bone. It is easy to understand not only the interconnection of each aspect but also the reliance of each on the other. Without sexual secretions we could not have a body in which blood nourishes flesh and bone.

As a goal, Taoists seek to restore the ching to its pure state, before masturbation ever took place, before sexual thoughts dominated our thought processes, and before anxiety took its toll on our lives. In part, it is the conservation of sexual secretions that restores and nourishes the blood. This restored blood, additionally nourished by proper diet and herbal medicines, and stimulated by the breath exercises, can then transform ching into its true or refined state.

Ching is also equated with the very force that drives us to procreate. Even though this energy can be very strong, Taoists do not view it as beneficial. Certain sects of Taoism, however, have mistakenly thought that restoring youthful vigor and the drive for sexual prowess were in themselves the restoration of ching. This erroneous belief entirely misses the point. That type of sexual energy is associated with fire (destructive) and creates the need for dissipation. Those who follow such methods get caught in a vicious circle of forever restoring and dissipating, which has nothing to do with forging the elixir.

It is because of such practices and misguided beliefs that competent teachers are such a necessity. A good teacher can supervise students so that they don't get caught up in this newfound sexual energy and end up destroying not only their ching but their qi and shen as well. These energies are interdependent, and if one is injured, they all suffer. Sexual prowess is not what the legitimate Taoist seeks; rather, it is sexual energy. The achievement of immortality comes through the forging and refining of the Three Treasures, not their dissipation.

Taoists understand quite clearly that it is because of sexual dissipation that we are in this world. Likewise it is the dissipation of ching that will cause our departure from the world. It is thus evident that if we conserve and nourish our ching, life itself can be preserved.

The immediate goal is to reach that state of both physical vitality and mental purity that we had as children. This does not mean that you immediately enforce celibacy upon yourself. "Natural celibacy," however, is the answer. Accomplished over time through the adherence of regulating body, breath, and mind, natural celibacy, the point where sexual desire just fades away and is no longer thought about, is achieved not by design but by the natural process of rejuvenation.

True restoration of ching is purely a benefit of someone who is focused on regulating the body; celibacy is by extension a result of the natural course of events. When the ching is restored, the notion of dissipation is feared, just as the notion of celibacy is feared by someone attached to sexual activity. No one should just jump into celibacy (which rarely produces the proper results anyway) and think that the problem will be solved. On the contrary, it will just create more problems, just as jumping into dual sexual-cultivation (Taoist practices in which men and women engage in sexual acts in order to form the elixir of immortality) will also create many problems.

An old story tells about a man who visits a Taoist mountain hermitage and becomes curious as to the comings and goings of the monks. He observes that the younger monks descend the mountain every month or so for a few days and assumes they fetch supplies in the town below. The middle-aged monks, he notices, descend about every six months. The elder monks and the three children who live there under their care never leave the mountain, even though the elders walk as spryly and with as much stamina as the children.

One evening at dinner, the man presents this observation to an elder monk, who responded as follows:

> The younger monks indeed fetch supplies, but also go to visit the 'flower girls' in town. They are still young and find celibacy too demanding and obstructive to their practices, so they need to dissipate every couple of months. Otherwise, sexual desire might dominate their thoughts and thus destroy their practice.

The middle-aged monks descend to take care of monastic business in town, but also on occasion to take advantage of the flower girls' favors, as every now and then the need for sex arises, but for them it is much less often than for the younger monks.

We elders live in repose from the duties of fetching supplies and business dealings. Besides, the walk is no longer worth the favors of the flower girls. Our minds are in keeping with the children, the only difference is that we elders are free of sexual attachment and the children not yet captured by it, but in the end it is the same.

Ching is restored, replenished, and accumulated by regulating the body through the practices of fasting, ingesting herbs, maintaining a certain diet, and exercises. These practices are aimed at restoring youth, vigor, strength, and stamina.

When we were young, we could seemingly play forever and never run out of energy. A day was an eternity when we were having fun. Summer vacation from school was beyond even the idea of an eternity. Time itself seemed slower in our youth. But as we grew older and had to deal with fear, anxiety, responsibility, sex, and so on, time also grew shorter with each passing year. In our adulthood, years and months race by like days, and days like minutes, rushing us faster and faster toward death. Taoists observed this passage of time and knew instinctively that a child's state of mind was far superior and more beneficial than an adult's. This is why the language of Taoism is filled with ideas and statements expressed, in English, with terms that begin with the prefix *re-* (restore, rejuvenate, regenerate, revert, regain, retain, return, refine, and so on). Taoism is forever referring to the "pliability of a child," as Lao-tzu called it.

Qi

Qi (breath) is rather complex, so it is difficult to provide a simple definition. Nonetheless, in regard to the arts of nourishing life, the basis for regulating the breath, we breathe in "primal breath" (yuan qi) from the atmosphere that in turn nourishes our "proper breath" (cheng qi). The more deeply and longer the breath can be held, the more primal breath is absorbed into the body, which then develops the

Qi

"true breath" (chen qi). True breath is generated by and from the lower abdomen. With this true breath the blood can be properly stimulated to circulate throughout the body, thus creating breath flow (yun qi). From this derives what is called "internal breath" (nei qi), which is the energy felt moving about the meridians and the source of heat felt in the body and its cavities. In other words, internal breath is the result of the proper practice of the arts of nourishing life or, more precisely, regulation of the breath (t'iao hsi).

Primal breath is the energy that permeates all things in the universe. It is what animates life and all substances. We breathe in this primal breath from the oxygen around us. The more primal breath that is absorbed into our bodies, the greater our level of spiritual attainment, physical and mental strength, and our ability to achieve longevity and immortality. So when the Taoists say, "sink the breath into the lower abdomen," they are speaking directly about the ability to absorb primal breath into the lower abdomen.

Proper breath is what nourishes our blood and body in normal daily life. This breath can be regulated to stimulate qi to a certain extent, but it can only provide short-term health benefits. It is not the qi used in forming the elixir of immortality. However, it is the qi used in external qigong—such as for breaking bricks—and through its development it can be transformed into true breath. True breath is the breath that permeates every element of the body. This is what Chuang-tzu meant by "a true man breathes through his heels." In the case of proper breath, the breath is manipulated physi-cally by the expansion and contraction of the abdomen and lungs. But true breath is driven by primal breath and is felt throughout the entire body. As an analogy, this is much like Lao-tzu's statement, "breathe like a bellows"; there is no place within the bellows that does not receive air. Experiencing this breath is unlike any other sensation of breathing. It is as if the entire body begins breathing in a very expansive, lively, and full manner, and yet it does so of its own accord. The body feels light, nimble, and active. Many practitioners can

I

experience this early on in their practice, but it usually occurs sporadically because the mental intention (called *i* in Chinese) is not yet strong enough.

True breathing comes not from pushing out the stomach and filling it with air, rather from focusing your attention and allowing the breath to follow mental intention. Anyone can accomplish this. Just close your eyes momentarily and focus your attention on your lower abdomen. Within moments you will feel the breath activated there. From this seemingly simple effort comes a wide range of qi development and experience. In *Pao-p'u-tzu*, Ko Hung states:

> Man exists within his breath, and breath is within man. Throughout Heaven, Earth, and the ten thousand things there is nothing which does not require breath to live. The man who knows how to circulate his breath can guard his own person and banish any evil which would attack him.

Numerous books, from those dealing with yoga and martial arts to those dealing with healing and meditation, have been written on the subject of breathing. It is rare, however, to find one that speaks about how the breath can really become natural and effective. Mostly these books speak about slowing the breath, making it deep, long, continuous, and even. Anyone who tries this soon discovers that the breath rises into the solar plexus and lung area and becomes short, tense, and unnatural. This happens because the breath is being *forced* to do something that it does not do naturally.

The breath has a rhythm of its own that should be allowed to slow down and become deep through the influence of the practice, not immediately and forcibly made to be slow and deep.

Another problem with the breath stems from how the abdomen itself is thought to function. Most people think that just pushing out the front of the abdomen is somehow abdominal breathing. This is only half breathing. The abdomen should be thought of as a balloon or bellows, with the entire area breathing, not just the front part.

Trying to make your breath slow, deep, continuous, and even is like stirring up a dirty glass of water to get the debris to settle; it will just continue to be muddled and agitated. If, however, the glass were set aside and left alone, the debris would settle to the bottom of the glass of its own accord.

As stated in the Mental elucidation of the thirteen kinetic postures (a t'ai chi ch'uan treatise attributed to the immortal ancestor Wang Chung-yueh):

> If you give all your attention to your intent [i] and ignore your breath [qi], your strength will be like pure steel. If, however, you only pay attention to the breath, the blood circulation will be obstructed and your strength weakened.

All you need to do in applying intent is to focus your attention on the lower abdomen (or whatever area you are working with) and the breath will follow. Sense and feel the area with all your attention. From this practice your breathing will naturally become slow, deep, continuous, and even because you are not trying to make it so; the breath is just acting in accord with the intent. This is truly "sinking the qi into the lower abdomen." Breath is like the debris in the glass of water; if you leave it alone, it will sink.

Another manner of explaining true breath is to refer to the idea of refinement. Breath that is concentrated low in the abdomen warms the blood, and blood that is warm circulates more completely. This warm blood then travels through the arteries in all the muscles of the body, and likewise is transported into all the veins that enter into all the sinews and tendons that surround the bones. From here the increased circulation and supply of blood reach not only the skin but actual bone through the capillaries. All the muscles, tendons, sinews, and skin are nourished by this warm blood. But more importantly, this warmed blood contains qi and enters the bone, turning it to marrow. When this occurs, the body again feels light, nimble, and active. This process restores the body, flesh, and bones to the pliability of a child's.

Another view of this is simply that the abdomen represents a cooking pot. Taoists clearly understood that the human body is made up mostly of fluids—water, blood, secretions, and so on—and fluids become stagnant unless mobilized. Water can be mobilized by heat, such as when it is boiled. Likewise, blood can be mobilized if heated. Taoists also understood that the breath is hot, and they associated it with fire. We blow on our cold hands to warm them, knowing the breath is hot. To a Taoist, then, the human body is like a large pot filled with water, and the breath is like the fire under the pot.

The abdomen contains bodily fluids, just as a cooking pot contains water. When the water is heated, it begins to move just as our blood moves when warmed and the breath is properly activated. Boiling water produces steam, just as our warmed blood produces qi. Into the water we place the uncooked (and thus inedible) rice so that we can eat it when it congeals into cooked rice. We likewise concentrate our breath on the lower abdomen, or, viewed in another way, on what can be called the emptiness of our abdomen. When the qi circulates (as in the cooking of rice), it congeals in the lower abdomen (thus making the rice edible) and is made functional.

This association of fire and water with abdominal breathing in Taoist practices is very important. When Taoists speak of fire and water (hou shui), they are referring to this process of breath heating and stimulating the ching (in the sense of blood). Achieving this important process is the purpose of all internal work.

Fire

This process of regulating the breath can be further compared to the refinement of ore into pure steel. The abdomen can be likened to the furnace; breathing to the bellows; qi to heat; and ching to ore. The more that ore is refined by blasting in the furnace, the more it can progress through the stages of turning into iron, iron into steel, and steel into pure steel. Ore turned into iron can be seen as the process of refining ching, iron turned into steel as the process of refining qi, and steel turned into pure steel as the process of refining shen.

But by definition, qi can also be associated with just about everything animate and inanimate. For example, the qi developed in martial arts to protect the body from injury is called defensive qi (wei qi). The qi derived from eating food for nourishment is called nourishment qi (ku qi). The qi inherited from your parents is called before heaven qi, and the qi you acquire from the arts of nourishing life practices is called after heaven qi. Indeed, even the weather is called heaven's qi (t'ien qi). All things in the universe have qi, from rocks to human beings. These different types of qi can be defined in terms of ten categories, three subtle and seven coarse, also referred to as the three heavenly spirits and the seven earthly spirits. The three subtle categories comprise the positive qi (ching, qi, and shen) and the seven coarse (seven emotions or passions) include the negative qi (happiness, joy, anger, grief, love, hatred, and desire).

Water

It is clear how extensively the concept of qi runs in Chinese thought. Qi is far more than just a latent energy abiding in the body. It encompasses all things in the universe, from stars to the tiniest dust motes.

Shen

Shen (spirit) manifests itself through intent. Only when
the ching and qi have united can there be shen. It is shen
that forges the mixture of ching and qi into the elixir,
or that moves the ching and qi in Nine Revolutions,   *Shen*
whereby a drop of pure spirit (these revolutions purify
and forge the essences of ching, qi, and shen into an elixir, a pill, or a seedlike
substance) can be deposited into the lower abdomen (Field of Elixir). This is
why the use of intent is so important in connection with leading the breath.
Shen is not just the mind or intention, no more than qi is just breathing or
ching is just blood circulation. Just as water can be transformed into steam,
intent can stimulate the breath to transform it into qi and blood into ching.
Shen can then transform this mixture (ching and qi) into the elixir.

The T'ai Chi Ch'uan Classic, attributed to the Sung dynasty (A.D. 960 to
A.D. 1126) Taoist immortal Chang San-feng, states, "The mind is the chief,
the qi is the banner, and the blood is the troops." In the old days of warring
in China, the chief would position himself on a hill to oversee the entire
battlefield. When he wanted to send his troops to a certain location, he would
first send his banner man there. Upon seeing the banner, the troops would
mobilize and go immediately to that place. This is likewise a description of
what is called moving the qi. Using mental intention, one sends the qi to
the location of an injury, and the blood (ching) then follows. When qi and
ching have congealed to undertake the task of healing the injury, we can say
that shen has manifested.

So, just as we can express our ching externally through numerous manners
of physical exertion, the qi can also be expressed externally through different
means. The shen, most powerful of all, can also be expressed externally in
countless ways. This state of external expression is called spirit illumination
(shen ming), and it means that the spirit can function and be utilized as
readily as the body.

The very heart of this practice is to create a spiritual embryo in which
the ching and qi can be thought of as the egg and sperm; intent brings
about the spiritual intercourse, and finally the child, shen. The lower
abdomen is the womb. Although the analogies used to explain ching, qi,
and shen might lead to the idea that they are mental phenomena, they are

indeed real physical phenomena, brought about through practice. Moreover, ching, qi, and shen are interdependent. When one becomes strengthened, the others benefit as well. When one is weakened, the others are likewise weakened. For this reason, a person needs to regulate the body, breath, and mind. Heaven has its three treasures: sun, moon, and stars. Earth has water, fire, and air. Human beings have ching, qi, and shen.

In each case, all three aspects must be kept in harmony for existence to be maintained. To see that this is true, all we need do is imagine what would happen to the heavens if the sun were to disappear, or to the earth if water were to vanish, or to a human being if he or she were to stop breathing. In all three cases, losing any one of the essential treasures would bring disaster to the whole. When our ching is depleted, the breath (qi) can function no more, and so the shen dissipates.

One of the rulers of the Shang dynasty (circa 1766 B.C. to 1154 B.C.) had engraved into all the imperial bathtubs, "Renew yourself every day completely, make yourself new daily, still anew today, and every day anew."

PART 2

THE EIGHT BROCADES— THE PHYSICAL PRACTICE

THE TRADITIONAL METHOD, WITH COMMENTARIES

AUTHOR'S INTRODUCTION TO THE EIGHT BROCADES

When I first began learning the eight seated qigong exercises known as the Eight Brocades, there was no single book written in English, or even Chinese, that could satisfy all my questions and doubts. I found only pieces to a puzzle, nothing comprehensive. This book, however, not only answers the questions I had during my initial years of attempting to learn the Eight Brocades correctly but also guides serious adherents safely into the wonderful realm of Taoist longevity theories—both their philosophies and their practices.

My practice of the Eight Brocades (in Chinese pa tuan chin, pronounced phonetically as "ba dwan jin") began in 1974 when my younger brother bought for me, on a whim, the *Taoist Health Exercise Book* by Da Liu. Although this book is primarily an introduction to the Taoist practices of t'ai chi ch'uan, meditation, philosophy, and herbs, it also provides instructions on the Eight Brocades exercises and gives a brief biography of Li Ching-yun (the reportedly 250-year-old Taoist who practiced the Eight Brocades). This work was my first introduction to Chinese Taoist longevity practices, and my interest has never waned since reading it and teaching myself the Eight Brocades exercises.

It was not until 1979, during my residency at the City of Ten Thousand Buddhas in Talmage, California, when I began to learn from a visiting monk, dharma master Chen Yi, how to perform the Eight Brocades correctly. Seeing him perform them confirmed that I had much to learn. His stay there was limited, as were my abilities to grasp what he was instructing. But I learned enough so that I could begin a more serious study and practice of this art.

In 1982 I was honored with the privilege of moving in with Master T. T. Liang and his family in St. Cloud, Minnesota. During my six-year residence there I translated every text on the Eight Brocades contained in his modest library. He likewise helped answer many questions I had about the Taoist arts of nourishing life. Also, he presented me with a copy of General Yang Shen's book of Li Ching-yun's life and practices, entitled An authoritative and authentic record of a highly respected 250-year-old man. Master Liang, who was a friend of Yang Shen, received one of the original copies of this book.

My translations of Li Ching-yun's introduction to the Eight Brocades exercises and his line-by-line commentary on the original text, presented in this section, are translated from Yang Shen's work. In Li's introduction and in each of the Eight Brocades sections, I have also provided my own commentary—under "Author's Comments"—to help clarify aspects of the text and expand on the ideas set forth in Li's commentary. I have also included detailed instructions with photographs showing the physical movements of the exercises.

The Development of the Eight Brocades

No matter the term used for Taoist longevity exercises, the intent is always the same: to stimulate and mobilize the internal energy of qi throughout the body. Mobilizing qi is the purpose and subject of the Eight Brocades.

History claims three popular inventors of the Eight Brocades. One theory says that T'ao Hung-ching, a Taoist adept of the fifth century A.D., created the exercises. Another says that Chung-li Ch'uan, one of the Eight Immortals, also of the fifth century A.D. and a follower of T'ao Hung-ching, invented them. And still another attributes their origin to the Taoist sage Chen Tuan (also know as Chen Hsi-yi, or sometimes as just Hsi-yi) of the tenth century A.D.

The first semblance of what is now known as the Eight Brocades appears in T'ao Hung-ching's *Hsiu shou chi* (Record on cultivating longevity). T'ao Hung-ching lived between A.D. 452 and A.D. 536, and he refers to the seated breath exercises (Tao yin exercises) as the Eight Forms (pa hsiang). Although the Record on cultivating longevity has been attributed to T'ao Hung-ch'ing, it is not certain that he actually authored it. It is thought that Chung-li Ch'uan, who studied with T'ao, received the transmission of these Eight Forms and possibly revised them as the Eight Brocades, then out of respect for his teacher attributed the work to him. It was a common practice in those times for students to attribute their own work to the teacher with whom they studied. This is difficult to verify but seems the most likely reason Chung-li Ch'uan is considered a founder of these exercises.

Other theories suggest that the Eight Brocades are a collection of various Taoist breath exercises with influences coming from the Buddhist patriarch Bodhidharma's works, the *I chin ching* and *Hsi sui ching* (Muscle changing classic and Marrow cleansing classic); or that the great Sung dynasty military leader General Yueh Fei invented the exercises. Each of these theories is very difficult to accept and prove. These two highly improbable founders serve more to validate the practice of the Eight Brocades within the Buddhist and martial arts schools.

The development of the Eight Brocades is rather clouded. All the various schools have claimed it as their own invention, and have inserted their own ideas. It has even been presented as twelve exercises, or the Twelve Brocades (shih erh tuan chin). The exercises also appear in a more dissected manner, with many additions, under the heading Internal Kung for the Four Seasons (nei kung szu ling), as twenty-four exercises for specific periods of the year. In martial arts, the Eight Brocades have become a system of not only standing postures but also sword and staff forms. They are now being presented as a form of qigong, a term that did not appear until 1910 in a book entitled *Shaolin tsung fa* (Shaolin orthodox methods). The author used the term generically to cover a wide range of ideas, including respiratory and meditative exercises directed at mobilizing the breath. Qigong is not in any sense a traditional Taoist term, but it has since been adapted to many Taoist works.

Since no clear evidence exists as to when the Eight Brocades were first developed, the answer as to their origin really depends on which school or thought of Taoism, Buddhism, Confucianism, medicine, or martial art you wish to believe. Each school seems to have its own unique evidence and prejudice.

A more practical view contends that the Eight Brocades are a product, both philosophically and physiologically, of Chinese culture since about

3000 B.C., drawing their philosophy from or around the ideas presented in the I Ching (Book of Changes) and the *Huang ti nei ching* (The Yellow Emperor's Classic of Internal Medicine). These exercises more likely developed over time through various phases rather than originating with a single creator, as Chinese "invented history" is so prone to suggest.

Suffice to say that the origin lies somewhere hidden in antiquity, and that until additional evidence is uncovered, it is better to view their origins as the result of a cumulative process. No matter how they developed, the Eight Brocades are unquestionably the culmination of Taoist alchemical exercises for health, longevity, and immortality.

Practicing and Finding a Teacher

If you want to be good at anything, you must do it every day. Great musicians play music every day, great writers write every day, great business people do business every day, and so on. Birds prove this as they fly every day. Birds don't say to themselves, "I think I won't fly for a few weeks," nor do they ever quit altogether. Birds fly every day, because it is their nature and purpose. Human beings should be healthy physically and spiritually because it is their nature and purpose to be so.

The Chinese have a term for practice, *lien hsi*. *Lien* means to refine, like in the refinement of ore into high-grade steel. It is the process of making something the best it can be. *Hsi* means to repeat, and the character that represents this word depicts the wings of a bird flapping continuously in front of the sun. Just as the sun comes up daily, to practice, or "flap your wings," should occur daily. And the inclusion of one stroke at the head of the character adds the idea of something simple and pure. So, to the Chinese mind, practice is something that retains the idea of repetition, like a bird flapping its wings to get from one place to another.

As the I Ching says, "Nature is in constant motion, so the activity of man should be to strengthen himself constantly." An ancient Chinese proverb likewise states, "A door pivot that is used never becomes worm eaten, and moving water never becomes stagnant and putrid."

If we want to have robust health and to prolong our life, then we must find a health maintenance practice to strengthen ourselves. Even though the Eight Brocades have a variety of health maintenance and enhancement therapies, caution must still be applied. It is wise to obtain a good teacher for supervised instruction. This is especially true if problems occur, and always if one has an illness. If the exercises are approached or practiced incorrectly, some of the following side effects can occur:

Constricted or unnatural breathing results from being hurried, anxious, or not keeping your breath out of the lung area, or from trying to be too precise and forceful with the breath. Let the breath be natural and calm and this will never be a problem.

Mental and physical exhaustion result from being too fanatical about the performance and training of the exercises. It can also result from forcing the breath to be deep and long. Again, breathe naturally and this problem never occurs.

Trance states can occur especially in the breathing exercises, and they may make you feel frozen and unable to breathe easily. The sensation is very akin to your entire body falling asleep and only the brain remaining active. Once it occurs, you may panic and struggle to shake it off, after which you might feel completely exhausted. Some people confuse this sensation with the heightened state of concentration called *samadhi—it is not at all the same thing*. Some practitioners can also have out-of-body experiences, which have no real value here whatsoever. You can prevent these problems by focusing on the method and not drifting off into scattered thoughts.

Increased sexual desire might result from abdominal breathing, which creates heat in the lower extremities and thus stimulates the sexual organs and the desire for sexual activity. Acting on that increased desire, however, will only result in dissipating the ching, which in turn depletes the qi and dulls the shen. One way of preventing this is by getting up and taking a walk outdoors in the fresh air and reminding yourself of the purpose of practice.

Uncontrollable reflex movement occurs from the muscles reacting to being motionless. Taoists compare this sensation to the idea that anything reaching its peak will automatically become its opposite. When yang reaches its peak, it becomes yin and vice versa. The body, when becoming too relaxed (yin), will become active (yang). Sometimes this side effect results in uncontrollable shaking or twitching. If this occurs, simply get up and take a walk or do some stretching.

Detoxification of the abdomen can provoke an increase in passing wind—which is not altogether bad because you are releasing unwanted toxins. Still, this is a side effect of a relaxed abdomen. A Chinese saying goes,

"One fart to an old man is worth one gold bar." Humorous but true. If we want to become healthier, we need to expel toxins. Another side effect can be rancid tasting saliva. Again, this is just another way in which the body extracts toxins. Don't be too concerned; both of these phenomena pass. However, if the breath smells or the saliva tastes like ammonia, then the liver might be misfunctioning for some reason and it is wise to see a physician.

Hallucinations result from two things, negative qi in the brain and a teacher who overly emphasizes psychic experience in his students rather than actual physical sensations. Negative qi results from students training too fast and feeling anxious about the results or achieving psychic experiences. Some teachers eager to make money and to acquire students don't provide the correct fundamentals for students and have them perform breathing exercises for too lengthy a time period, or they simply don't know how to help them advance properly. You can prevent hallucinations by progressing gradually and finding a competent teacher.

Fanaticism is probably the most common side effect. It stems mostly from having a teacher who doesn't keep you focused on the method rather than on your personal accomplishments. It is very easy for your ego to become inflated, and when you experience a little qi you may think you are a master or have illusionary thoughts of being spiritually superior. There are more things in this world than the Eight Brocades, and there are more things in this world than just your qi and ego. Lao-tzu understood this when he claimed that his three treasures were frugality, compassion, and humility. Avoid fanaticism by following Lao-tzu's example.

Many teachers spend an inordinate amount of time preaching the dangers of qigong, but dangers only come from being taught incorrectly. The qigong world is filled with charlatans and you should pick your teacher with great caution. In fact, Ko Hung advised that more care should be given to the choice of a teacher than to the method. Ninety-nine percent of all qigong students fail to develop qi, not because of the method but because of their teacher's inability to produce qi in him- or herself.

Master Liang had fifteen very competent teachers, yet he met many others who were not genuine. He always advised that you should try to get teachers to prove some of their skill before you study with them. Can they produce extreme heat in their hands? Can they hold their breath for long periods without strain? Can they transfer qi to you? Do they have physical marks of concentrated qi—reddened areas on the back of the head, on the chest, or on the hands (palms or fingers)? If a teacher has truly acquired qi, he or she can meet the above minimal requirements.

Also, do not assume seeming psychic abilities mean that true qi is also present. Too many teachers feign psychic skills to conceal their lack of genuine qigong accomplishment. As the old saying goes, "No one can give you something they don't have." So in the end, find a good, competent teacher and you will never suffer any of the above side effects.

Li Ching-yun

In A.D. 1678, during the reign of Kang Hsi, the second emperor of the Manchu dynasty (which lasted from A.D. 1644 to A.D. 1908), Li Ching-yun was born. His birthplace was in Kuei-chou province, a mountainous region of southwestern China. His family later moved north to Szechuan province.

Li Ching-yun is probably the oldest documented man to have ever lived, living a remarkable 250 years. He is not the figment of anyone's imagination nor part of China's "invented history." Yet, to ascertain his exact age at death has proven difficult. However, even if the surveys conducted by the Chinese government authorities erred to the extent of fifty years, which is not improbable, he would still be historically the oldest human being on record.

Li Ching-yun

Again, Li Ching-yun is not a myth by any means. There are numerous family records and accounts of his life documented by Chinese officials, friends, and disciples. Government officials, after Li's death, conducted investigations to verify his true age and concluded that he indeed had lived to be well over 250 years of age.

It is documented that Li married fourteen times in succession and has 180 descendants covering a span of eleven generations. Many of the oldest men in his district could remember stories of him related by their own grandfathers, some of whom were disciples or acquaintances of Li.

In 1927, General Yang Shen, upon hearing of this incredible man, sought out Li's whereabouts and invited him to visit Wanhsien. Li accepted and remained there for nearly two years. It was during this time that Yang Shen began compiling a book based on the teachings of Li, which were contained in the transcripts of twenty-eight, three-hour lectures given by Li at the University in Wanhsien. The book in its entirety addresses many subjects, such as meditation, breathing, internal cultivation, moral deportment, and philosophy. General Yang Shen describes Li in his book in the following excerpt:

> Master Li is nearly 250 years old, yet I have seen him stride spryly through the mountains, and his younger companions find it quite difficult to keep up with his quick pace. His height is well over six feet. His skin has a very rosy complexion and his head is completely bald, but very shiny. He also keeps his fingernails very long. In one meal I've seen him eat three or more bowls of rice, seasoned with chicken or other types of meat. For good health, Li always advised to walk lightly and avoid tension.

General Yang Shen was a very wealthy warlord from Szechuan province. It was during the year 1930 that he began compiling the lectures and teachings of Li Ching-yun into a book, publishing it under the title of *Erh pai wu shih shui jen chui shih chi* (An authoritative and authentic record of a highly respected 250-year-old man). This was later revised and published in 1970 by Li Huan and Yu Cheng-sheng in Taiwan. Yang Shen himself lived to be ninety-eight years old and was also a very avid mountain climber throughout most of his life.

For the major portion of his life Li Ching-yun lived in the mountainous regions of northern China, predominantly in the O-mei regions of Szechuan province. There he wandered about collecting herbs and teaching his disciples. When he could no longer comfortably carry the herbs he collected, he would take them into the local villages and sell them at inexpensive rates. He did not like being too profit minded, and his attitude created goodwill between himself and the vendors. He considered this business attitude the best, as everyone was kept happy.

Throughout his life Li had various occupations, even that of soldier. Yet for the most part, he sold medicinal herbs and taught many disciples the secrets of long life and youthfulness, some of whom lived to be more than one hundred years of age themselves.

In the year 1808, at the age of 130, Li explains that while roaming the Kung Tung mountains of Kansu province, he met a Taoist hermit who was well over 500 years old, having been born in 1270 A.D. He gives special claim to the fact that this teacher taught him a set of internal exercises that he called the Methods of the Eight Diagram Active Kun (pa kua hsing kung fa). It was these exercises that Li credited with his remarkable longevity. For nearly one hundred years he performed these exercises daily. But, as he also explained, without proper living habits and disciplines, physical as well as spiritual, all would be in vain. The mind and body, he instructed, must be cultivated as a unit, not as two separate entities.

While residing with General Yang Shen, Li permitted his photograph to be taken, and this is the only known photograph of him. The photo advanced his popularity throughout China, and soon his fame was widespread. When the populace learned of his presence in Wanhsien, many traveled there just to have a look at him. Most visitors could not speak his dialect, but they were content with having had the opportunity to gaze upon his face. Large sums of money were donated by some in order to ensure just a brief appointment with him.

Shortly after Li Ching-yun left Wanhsien in 1930, Yang Shen gave a copy of Li's photograph to Generalissimo Chiang Kai-shek, who then requested an audience with the immortal. Unfortunately, Yang Shen's envoy who sought out Li's whereabouts reported that the venerable Li had passed away. It was claimed that Li died of natural causes at the age of 256. The envoy, however, felt that his death was a hoax created by his closest disciples, designed to protect Li from any further public contact. It was speculated that Li was living in a very remote part of northwestern China, under the protection of wealthy disciples and a Taoist hermitage. Li himself frequently instructed disciples not to live in cities and among worldly men, as it would shorten one's years. Whatever the case may be, the news of Li's death even reached the *New York Times,* further testimony of how widespread his fame had become.

On June 5, 1928, the *Northern China Daily Newspaper* of Shanghai ran the following article:

250 YEARS OLD

And still doing well! Wonder man of Szechuan!

The accompanying portrait, taken in the spring of last year, is that of Master Li Ching-yun, an old and respected resident of Shangchun Village in Kaihsien, a place to the north of Wanhsien, China. Born in the seventeenth year of the reign of Kang Hsi, the second emperor of the Manchu dynasty, Master Li is now in his 250th year. In spite of his years he is very young and vigorous in spirit and he is physically strong. His facial appearance is no different from others two centuries his junior.

A native of Chingnan, he has traveled widely, and everywhere he goes the people welcome him. Numerous military and civil leaders have conferred honors and presents upon him.

When he was only a few years old he could read and write. He traveled throughout Shensi, Kansu, Sinkiang, Manchuria, Tibet, Annam, and Siam, gathering various herbs. This continued to be his trade until he was about 200 years old. Some of his traveling companions at this time were even older than himself.

Master Li has many disciples, all of whom are men of venerable age. Some of the oldest men in his district say that their grandfathers knew him. Disciples, when questioned, say that Master Li taught them to keep a quiet heart by "sitting like a tortoise and walking sprightly like a bird, and to sleep like a dog."

The longevity exercises of Huang Lao may have been burnt, but Master Li still lives on and his teachings may lead others to learn how to lengthen their years.

The next chapter of Part 2 contains Li Ching-yun's introduction to the original text of the Eight Brocades, text that comes from a stone engraving by Kao Lin in Hangchou in the late 1600s. Interspersed through the introductory text by Li are my own comments and translation of the Kao Lin text. The remaining chapters in Part 2 detail each of the Eight Brocades exercises and include the original Kao Lin text, comments by Li and me, and my detailed instructions on how to do each of the exercises. The final chapter in Part 2 presents concluding exercises and Kao Lin's comments taken from the original Kao Lin engraving. The drawings that introduce each brocade are by Master Ching Lai, and they first appeared in a text printed during the Ching dynasty (A.D. 1644 to A.D. 1908) by Cheng Kung-ying of Hsiang Shan Ssu (Fragrant Hill Monastery).*

*Note: The "Ching dynasty" and the "Manchu dynasty" are two different names for the same time period.

It is strongly advised to practice in the described manner for at least three months of daily practice before incorporating the supplementary techniques outlined in Part 3 of the book (with the exception of the Externally Patting the Eight Subtle Meridians and Twelve Cavities regime). Before working through the Lesser Heavenly Circuit regime, however, make sure that you have practiced the second regime, Internally Opening the Eight Subtle Qi Cavities, paying particular attention to the comments about the Lesser Earthly and Lesser Human circuits.*

*There are two primary ways in which to stimulate the qi in the body, the external and the internal. External stimulation consists of actual physical methods (such as patting), while internal stimulation is mental (meditation). This distinction gives rise to the Taoist concepts of *Wai Dan* (the external methods for producing the elixir of immortality) and *Nei Dan* (the internal methods).

Li Ching-yun's Introduction to the Original Text of the Eight Brocades

A translation of Li Ching-yun's introduction to the Eight Brocades follows, interspersed with my comments and translation of the original text of the Eight Brocades.

The Methods of the Eight Diagram Active Kung

I call these methods active kung. My teacher handed down these exercises to me as the Methods of the Eight Diagram Active Kung.

Author's Comments

Active kung (hsing kung) is a fairly common term found in qigong, meditation, and martial arts Chinese texts. Normally it is translated simply as "exercises." The term *hsing* can mean "activity" or "practice"; *kung* translates as "skill," "work," or "effort." This *kung* is the same as in *kung fu*. However, the Taoist meaning of *hsing kung* is closer to the idea of "practicing yoga."

The reason that the term *Eight Diagram* (pa kua) is used here can be assumed to have been in order to establish a correlation with the I Ching Eight Diagram theory. However, the problem is that Li Ching-yun does not attempt any effort at explaining these correlations. Maybe his teacher related them to him, but Li did not share them in his lectures.

The first emperor of China, Fu Hsi, supposedly invented the Eight Diagrams during the legendary period of the Age of the Five Rulers, approximately 3000 B.C. The Eight Diagrams are composed of eight sets of three straight- or broken-lined images that represent our phenomenal world. These eight three-lined images are the very basis on which yin yang theory is founded, with the yang forces represented by solid lines and the yin forces by broken ones. In a vision, Fu Hsi saw the Eight Diagrams on the back of a tortoise shell. From these eight images, he divined and perceived the natural changes occurring in the world. Later, other emperors, for purposes of divination, would drill holes into tortoise shells, burn them, and then, by the cracks produced, determine the images pertinent to their questions. Dried bones of dead animals were also used for these purposes.

Over the course of China's history, these eight images developed into an entire system of divination and philosophy. Other than the Five Activities (wu hsing) theories, nothing has been more important to the early Chinese mind than the Eight Diagrams. If a philosophy, health practice, martial art, or medical theory cannot be equated with or validated by the Eight Diagrams or Five Activities, it really has little worth in the Chinese mind.*

During the Chou dynasty (1122 B.C. to 255 B.C.), King Wen stacked the Eight Diagrams on top of each other to create the sixty-four six-lined images, or hexagrams, that we see in the Book of Changes today. His son, the Duke of Chou, formulated many of the meanings of the sixty-four images. Subsequently, Confucius and some of his later disciples added their commentaries, ending with what is now called the "Ten Wings" of the I Ching.

---

*The Five Activities, which are sometimes referred to as the Five Elements or Attributes (metal, wood, water, fire, and earth), is a central theory in Chinese philosophy that codifies how all phenomena act and behave. The reason I choose the term "The Five Activities" is that it is not so much the element itself that is important, but the element's associated activity. For example, fire is not only heat producing; it also creates light, and it can cause changes in the other four elements as well. So it is the phenomenon of one element's effect upon the others that creates the idea of "activity." Also, the Chinese term *wu hsing* literally means "five activities." The term "Elements" is really a contrived term here; at best this theory could be called the "Five Element Activities" or "Activities of the Five Elements."

It would be impossible to fully delve into Eight Diagram theory here. Suffice to say that these eight images all relate to the Eight Brocades in that the images pertain to the exercises, as well as to qi cavities and meridians, as shown in Part 3.

The Eight Diagrams predate the creation of the Eight Brocades. However, no one is sure whether or not the exercises were originally called Eight Brocades or Eight Diagrams. The assumption is that Li Ching-yun's teacher (and maybe his whole lineage succession before and after him) chose to call the exercises "Methods of the Eight Diagram Active Kung." It may have also been that Li's teacher was able to study the original silks (brocades) of Ma-wang-tui, and so made the connection between the eight exercises presented on them and the eight diagrams of the I Ching. It also may have been that the exercises were originally associated with the eight diagrams and later put on the silks without reference to the eight diagrams. The point, though, is that they do correlate and Li Ching-yun, interestingly enough, was the first person to reveal the correlation and claim that the Eight Brocades can in fact be equally called the Eight Diagram exercises.*

In the Fu Hsi arrangement of these eight images, we find the following correlations to the Eight Brocades practice:

Heaven (Ch'ien), south, the Hundred Gatherings cavity (pai hui, top of the head), corresponds to the First Brocade, the Heavenly Drum.

Thunder (chen), northeast, the Ocean of Qi cavity (qi hai, lower abdomen), corresponds to the Second Brocade, Shake the Heavenly Pillar.

Valley (tui), southeast, the Mysterious Pass cavity (hsuan kuan, between the eyes), corresponds to the Third Brocade, the Red Dragon Stirs the Sea.

Water (k'an), west, the Double Pass cavity (shuang kuan, middle of the back), corresponds to the Fourth Brocade, Rub the Court of the Kidneys.

---

*There is another important point here. There have been persons within the martial art world who have claimed that Li Ching-yun trained in the martial art of *Pa Kua Chang* (Eight Diagram Palms). But nothing in his lectures or life points to him having known any martial art technique. It may be that persons have misconstrued his practice of Eight Diagram Active Kung (Eight Brocades) with that of Eight Diagram Palms.

Fire (li), east, the Bright Palace cavity (chiang kung, solar plexus), corresponds to the Fifth Brocade, the Single Pass Windlass.

Wind (sun), southwest, the Jade Pillow cavity (yu chen, back of the head), corresponds to the Sixth Brocade, the Double Pass Windlass.

Mountain (ken), northwest, the Gates of Life cavity (ching men, kidney region), corresponds to the Seventh Brocade, Supporting Heaven.

Earth (K'un), north, the Returning Yin cavity (hui yin, perineum region), corresponds to the Eighth Brocade, Grasping with Hooks.

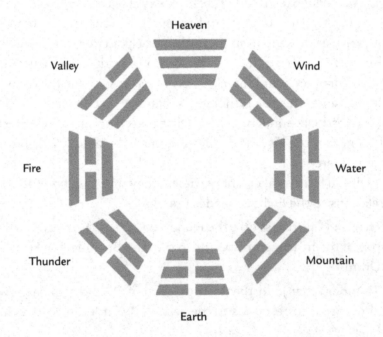

The Fu Hsi arrangement of the Eight Diagrams

The fundamental purpose here for the Eight Brocade correlations to the Eight Diagrams rests in the fact that the Chinese have always seen the human body as a microcosmic image of the larger, macrocosmic universe. Human beings are but an archetype of heavenly beings and heavenly structure. The Eight Diagrams are the macrocosmic patterns from which all things (heaven, earth, and man) are created. So as heaven has phenomena that reflect or symbolize each of the eight images, so do earth and man.

The Eight Diagrams are a symbolic representation of the physiological process that restores man's natural essences of ching, qi, and shen.

For when the Eight Diagrams are in their correct positions, heaven's natural essences (sun, moon, and stars) and earth's (fire, water, and air) are also in perfect harmony.

These exercises can be performed by anyone as they are very simple. They are regarded as *tao yin* methods. The secrets of these exercises are versed:

Author's Comments
The secrets that follow are included in the original text of the Eight Brocades.

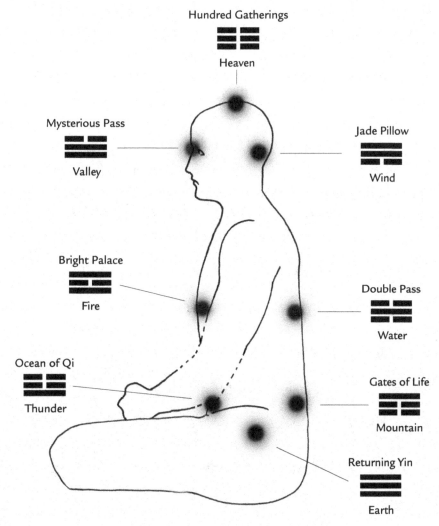

The Eight Diagram relationship to the body

Secrets of the Eight Brocades

Seated cross-legged, close the eyes to darken the heart.

Grasp the hands firmly and meditate on the spirit.

Tap the teeth thirty-six times.

The two hands embrace K'un-lun Shan.

Left and right, beat the Heavenly Drum,

Sounding it twenty-four times.

Gently shake the Heavenly Pillar.

The Red Dragon stirs up the saliva;

Rouse and rinse the saliva thirty-six times.

Evenly fill the mouth with Divine Water;

Each mouthful is divided into three parts and swallowed.

When the dragon moves, the tiger flees.

Stop the breath and rub the hands until hot;

On the back massage the Gates of Life.

Entirely exhaust one breath;

Imagine the heat aflame at the Navel Wheel.

Left and right, turn the Windlass.

Stretch out both feet loosely;

Afterward both hands support the Void.

Repeatedly bend the head over and seize the feet.

Wait for the saliva to be produced;

Rinse and swallow, dividing it into three parts;

Altogether swallow the Divine Water nine times.

Swallow it down with the sound of ku ku;

Then the hundred pulses will be naturally harmonized.

Complete the motion of the River Cart.

Direct the fire to circulate and heat the entire body.

The purpose of these exercises is to prevent harmful influences from approaching, to provide clearness during sleep and in dreams, to prevent cold and heat from entering, and to keep pestilence from encroaching.

These exercises are best practiced between the hours of Tzu and Wu, as doing so will create harmony between Ch'ien and K'un and will establish their proper connection with each other within the cyclic arrangement [of the Eight diagrams]. Hence, everything connected to [the procedures of] restoring one's original nature and returning to the Tao has excellent reasoning.

Author's Comments

Close the eyes to darken the heart is a very common phrase in all Taoist works. Close the eyes simply means to shut the eyes so that the mind will not be disturbed by external distractions. To a Taoist, however, closing the eyes can be performed in one of three manners. The first is described as "lowering the bamboo curtains," which does not mean completely closing the eyes; rather, the eyelids are lowered to the point where just a bit of light still comes through—in the same way that light passes through a bamboo screen. The attention then is placed on the darkened area just above the light, which will prevent sleepiness and distraction. The second type of closing the eyes is to gaze at the tip of the nose, but again with the eyes mostly closed with just a bit of light coming through. The attention of both eyes is placed on the tip of the nose and into the darkness just beyond it. The third way, which also lets in a little light, focuses on rolling the eyes back and slightly upward, without straining the eyeballs. You imagine that you are looking up into the top of the head (the Hundred Gatherings cavity) or a point between the eyes and back one inch (the shang tan t'ien), looking for a brightness within the darkness.

Darken the heart (ming hsin) refers to the darkness created by lowering the eyelids. When you lower your eyelids, you will experience in your eyes a definite line of light and darkness. It is this darkness on which your attention should be focused. Ming means dark, obscure, or profound; hsin means both heart and mind, the two being synonymous in Chinese thought and language. When translating this term into English, I have usually used the word *heart* in order to place more emphasis on the idea of will or intent and less on the concept of rational thinking, which the word *mind* often implies.

Here the term *restoring and returning* is a reference to cultivating qigong as a means of returning to the Tao, or more simply, a reference to spiritual self-cultivation.

Li includes the following eight-part song in his commentary, but it is not in fact part of the original text.

AN EIGHT-PART SONG
IN PRAISE OF THE EIGHT BROCADES

Massaging with warm hands and making use of the saliva produce a beautiful facial appearance.

Author's Comments
Massaging with warm hands is a reference to dry bathing, which consists of massage exercises that imitate the actions of bathing. *Making use of the saliva* refers to using the tongue to massage the cheeks and gums.

Pushing up the palms and shaking the head result in the ears not becoming deafened.

Author's Comments
Pushing up the palms refers to the Seventh Brocade, Supporting Heaven. *Shaking the head* is another exercise of dry bathing.

Cultivating the two hands to a high level can remove all obstacles.

Author's Comments
The two hands become the expression of qi when you cultivate to the degree of being able to consciously will qi. In part this means the ability to generate extreme heat in the hands, which can be used for healing.

It is wrong in principle, if, when pounding the body, it causes aching or pain.

Author's Comments
Pounding the body is a reference to using a pestle, a bag of pebbles, or a wooden pestle to knead the body. (See the Externally Patting the Eight Subtle Meridians and Twelve Cavities regime in Part 3.)

Massaging the soles of the feet until hot will make for lively walking.

Author's Comments
This exercise is found in the Eighth Brocade, Grasping with Hooks.

Pulling the Windlass means to be free of the work of changing the muscles and tendons.

Author's Comments
This is a reference to the *I chin ching* (muscle changing classic), attributed to the Buddhist patriarch Bodhidharma.

Gazing fiercely like a tiger and arching the back regulates the wind.

Author's Comments
Wind refers to the breath.

With proper breathing, the five viscera can all be void of any harmful afflictions.

Author's Comments
For the viscera (heart, lungs, kidneys, liver, spleen), there is not only a proper breathing method to strengthen them but a sound, color, and exercise as well.

Within the exercises of the Eight Brocades, and implied above in Li's eight-part song, you'll find that eight very distinct types of therapeutic methods are applied. The very heart of these therapies lies in enhancing your ability to sense and feel the inner and outer workings of body and mind. Once you establish a foundation of increased sensitivity to yourself, then the subtle inner energies of ching, qi, and shen can not only be experienced but also be consciously applied.

    The first therapy is the method of massage, such as the patting and pressing aspect of the Heavenly Drum, the pressing activity in Shake the Heavenly Pillar, the rubbing of the kidneys and heating of the hands in

Rub the Court of the Kidneys, and the massaging of the Bubbling Well (yung ch'uan) cavities in Grasping with Hooks.

The second is the use of sound, as in the tapping of the Heavenly Drum, listening to the breath, hearing the sound of *ku ku,* and using the five half coughs.

The third is the therapy of visualization, as in imagining a fire burning in the lower abdomen, producing light in the Jade Pillow cavity, or imagining the qi circulating in the body.

The fourth is the method of twisting and stretching, as seen in Shake the Heavenly Pillar, the Single Pass Windlass and Double Pass Windlass, Supporting Heaven, and Grasping with Hooks.

The fifth is the method of breath control, of which four main types are used: cleansing breath (ching hsi), natural breathing (tzu hsi), tortoise breathing (kuei hsi), and stopping the breath (pi qi).

Cleansing breath involves breathing in through the nose and exhaling through the mouth while making an aspirated *ha* or *ho* sound. This type of breathing aids in ridding the body of any impurities in the nose, lungs, and throat. It is usually performed nine times with any type of qigong exercise.

Ha is one of the Six Healing Sounds, part of a practice common to almost all Taoist traditions. The sounds are *ha, hu, shi, hisss, shu,* and *fu.* Each sound should be produced during exhalation with a noticeable aspiration. Made from the lower abdomen as it contracts and pushes the air upward, the sounds vibrate and pass through the throat—but do not come from there. *Ha* is used to heal the heart. While sitting, place the hands, with fingers intertwined, behind the head and utter *ha* thirty-six times. *Hu* cures the spleen. While sitting, place the hands over the tan-t'ien area (the lower abdomen) and pronounce the *hu* sound thirty-six times. *Shi* cures the solar plexus. While sitting, place the hands over the kidney area and sound *shi* thirty-six times. *Hisss* cures the lungs. While standing, intertwine the fingers behind the head and utter *hisss* thirty-six times. *Shu* cures the liver. While sitting, place the hands, fingers intertwined, behind the head and utter *shu* thirty-six times. If the abdomen is overly warm, lie down on the back with eyes closed and sound *shu* thirty-six times. *Fu* cures the kidneys. Sit on the floor, place the arms around the knees with the fingers intertwined, and pronounce the sound *fu* thirty-six times.

Natural breath is breathing through the nose only. During the inhalation, as the abdomen naturally expands, attention is focused on feeling the expansion of breath at the lower spine as well. On the exhalation, as the abdomen contracts, attention is paid to the contraction of the front of the lower abdomen. Natural breathing occurs though intent. Focusing on these areas will help you work your entire abdomen and allow you to push up air naturally through the diaphragm and into the lung area. Gradually, you will be able to feel the inhalation rise up from the lower spine to the middle of the back, and then feel it sink, on the exhalation, from the solar plexus down into the lower abdomen. This cannot be made to happen physically, or externally, by forcing the expansion or contraction with the muscles. You must allow it to happen naturally, and internally, by paying attention and applying your mental intention.

The use of mental intention in connection with the breath plays a very important role in holding the breath and in tortoise breathing. In holding the breath, it is the mental intention that leads the breath through the Function and Control meridians (the Lesser Heavenly Circuit) to locations of injury or pain. In tortoise breathing, mental intention leads the swallowed breath (as well as the swallowed saliva) down into the lower abdomen. The whole notion of using mental intention—at first through your imagination—is of utmost importance.

Holding the breath, or *embryonic breathing,* takes on several forms in the Eight Brocades practice. For one, you hold the breath while counting heartbeats, usually twelve (in advanced practice, the number would be sixty, one hundred twenty, or one thousand). For another, you hold the breath for two heartbeats after completing the inhalation and then count your heartbeats (twelve or more) while performing the exhalation referred to in the texts as "exhausting one breath completely." You also hold the breath when heating the hands for massage. And finally you hold the breath in order to either lead qi to a specific area or circulate it through the meridians.

In order to guide the qi when holding the breath, you should practice applying the Four Activities: (1) draw in the anus; (2) place the tongue on the roof of the mouth, thus forming what is called the "magpie bridge"; (3) close the eyelids and roll the eyes upward and back to visualize the Hundred Gatherings or Jade Pillow cavities—don't strain the eyes, just look back as far as you comfortably can; and (4) inhale slowly and after a complete inhalation, hold the breath for twelve or more heartbeats. As you hold your breath, imagine the qi moving up from the Returning Yin cavity to the Hundred Gatherings cavity. (The locations of these cavities and how to practice acquiring qi in them are explained in Part 3.)

Tortoise breathing is the process of what is sometimes called ingesting qi or saliva. This is applied in the Red Dragon Stirs the Sea brocade and in the Lesser Heavenly Circuit regime described in Part 3. Tortoise breathing should be combined with the Four Activities. With the fists raised above the head (see the instructions for the Third Brocade), and after holding the breath and imagining the qi moving up to the Hundred Gatherings cavity, swallow the air or saliva, and exhale, sensing the the qi or saliva dropping down into the lower abdomen (tan t'ien).

The reader should note that *reverse breathing* is not applied in the Eight Brocades, nor is it used in most Taoist practices (or "soft" styles of martial arts). Found predominately in the kung fu or "hard" styles of martial arts, reverse breathing is the opposite of natural breathing. In reverse breathing, the abdomen is contracted on inhalation and expanded on exhalation. Reverse breathing accentuates the external expression or aspects of qi but does little in the way of actual internal accumulation of qi. And, unless you have accumulated sufficient qi, reverse breathing has little function and can cause negative side effects internally. Because the inhalation works in conjunction with contracting the abdomen, the breath is sent high into the upper back and shoulders, and into the head—which can cause many problems. Do not perform reverse breathing with these exercises. All of my teachers have unanimously advised not to bother with reverse breathing. Master Liang referred to it as "big-head breathing" because more often than not that is the end result.

The sixth therapy is that of swallowing, which begins with the saliva and later includes the breath itself.

The seventh therapy is the use of meditative techniques.

And the eighth therapy is the circulation of qi through the Function and Control meridians (the Lesser Heavenly Circuit).

The therapies and exercises of the Eight Brocades can lead you far along the path of learning how to take care of yourself. If you can discipline yourself and practice each day, you will notice over time an incredible difference in your vitality and sense of well-being. Later on, as you continue to improve your concentration and become more adept at the exercises, the rewards will be even greater, both physically and spiritually.

In the verses above, we can observe the methods of the Eight Diagram Active Kung [Eight Brocades], which really are the very best and most wondrous methods for invigorating the body. Yet, most people, because of their life situations, even if they obtain these verses and songs, are unable to understand their profound meaning. Because of this, they live in contradiction of what is natural. It would be wise for them to begin by putting forth every effort into these exercises, so that they will no longer suffer and toil their lives away. Some will want to practice only during their leisure time, but this type of training is insufficient. Alas! How unfortunate the result, as these types of persons only bring about their early and hurried death.

Author's Comments
Li Ching-yun always referred to the Eight Brocades as the "Eight Diagram Active Kung," so I have chosen to preserve that terminology when translating his voice.

Formerly, when my master first considered me able enough to teach these exercises, I found their principles to be beyond my comprehension: so subtle and abstruse, limitless and yet of one nature, but different in form. However, I did understand that they could aid society and benefit the minds of all people. After a time, I found the desire to teach.

Once, I asked my teacher why he had not previously dared to transmit these teachings to others, especially to other Taoist sects. His response was:

Because those in the various sects obtain teachings and then change them according to their liking and to suit the tenets of their sect. They in turn go on to transmit them to others; then these persons change them again to their liking and proceed to transmit them—too much of the original teaching is then discarded and lost. Therefore, I am giving you the responsibility of imparting these teachings correctly. You must transmit them as broadly as possible, for if only one person were able to practice these exercises, then only one person would attain a good old age. If only one thousand and eight persons practice these exercises, then only that many persons would acquire health in old age. However, by widely transmitting this profound Tao of living beyond one hundred years, all the people of China would be able to attain a good old age, and all the people of the ancient state of the great Han could also have attained a good old age as a nation.

Author's Comments

Perhaps an explanatory note is necessary here to bring Li's meaning into focus. What he is saying is that if all the Hans (which was Li's race) had begun practicing the Eight Brocades when he did, during the time when the Hans ruled China, rather than the Manchus, they would all still be alive, and by extension, so would the great ancient state of the Han people.

Therefore, the following commentary on the original text of the Eight Brocades is given so that these teachings can be widely transmitted to the various Taoist sects. For herein lie the secrets, explained line by line, that reveal the subtle knowledge contained in these exercises. This commentary will, it is hoped, aid everyone in practicing the Eight Diagram Active Kung [Eight Brocades] in the proper sequence, and impart a correct understanding of the procedures so that all may realize their completion.

THE FIRST BROCADE

THE HEAVENLY DRUM

This chapter begins with my translation of the instructions, commentary, and correct method that were included in the Kao Lin engraving. Following the original text are Li Ching-yun's commentary and my comments, and finally my instructions for practicing the First Brocade.

The Original Text

Seated cross-legged, close the eyes to darken the heart.

Grasp the hands firmly and meditate on the spirit.

Tap the teeth thirty-six times.

The two hands embrace K'un-lun Shan.

> *The two hands are placed on the back of the head. Breathe nine times without sound through the nose, so that neither the in breath nor the out breath can be heard.*

Left and right, beat the Heavenly Drum,

Sounding it twenty-four times.

> *Position the hands so that they cover both ears. Press the middle finger against the index finger and then tap downward against the back of the head, alternating left and right, twenty-four times on each side.*

> ***The correct method:*** *First, it is necessary to close the eyes to darken the heart, cross the legs, grasp the hands firmly, and still the thoughts. Afterward, tap the teeth thirty-six time to collect the spirit. Next, place both hands on the back of the head and take nine breaths that cannot be heard, using the secret of the hands to cover both ears. Next, beat the Heavenly Drum by pressing the middle finger over the index finger, and begin tapping the back of the head, left and right, twenty-four times.*

Li Ching-yun's Commentary

Closing the eyes will, in effect, nourish the spirit, and darkening the heart is necessary to control the false thinking.

After you are seated, the procedure is to securely close the eyes to focus inwardly. All the confused thoughts will begin to vanish and return into the darkness; the mind can then thoroughly and intuitively illuminate all things.

When sitting in the cross-legged position, do so on a thick cushion. The head must be held upright and the spine kept erect. Your entire being can then enter the Four Dhyanas, self-reliant and independent in all things. The tailbone must also be kept upright, not leaning to one side or another. This is very important.

Author's Comments

In Taoism the term *ching tso* is used, and it means tranquil sitting. The purpose of quiet sitting is suggested by the image of a glass of water with debris floating in it. If the glass is left unmoved, the debris will naturally sink to the bottom of the glass, leaving the top portion clean and clear. Thus, the more calmly you sit, the more your thoughts will settle and the greater will be your experience of a clean and clear mind. The great Japanese Zen master Dogen maintained that the most important part in becoming a Buddha had to do with sitting like a Buddha, being ever mindful of correcting your sitting posture, and nothing more.

The proper method of sitting for the Eight Brocades is the *siddha* posture, a cross-legged posture that has the left heel tight up against the base of the genital area and the right leg aligned in front so that the sole of the foot rests along the left knee. However, you may also use the half-lotus or full-lotus posture. If you are physically unable to perform any of these seated postures, you can sit on the edge of a chair instead, as long as your back is straight and not supported by the chair.

All the confused thoughts will begin to vanish and return into the darkness. The idea here is that first the mind is full of confused thoughts and images. When all the confused thoughts vanish and return into the darkness, the mind settles and emptiness fills with light, which is the meaning of *the mind can then thoroughly and intuitively illuminate all things.* Returning to the analogy of the glass of dirty water, the debris represents the confused thoughts. When the glass is left perfectly still, there comes a point at which the water is murky but still. Last, the debris eventually sinks to the bottom of the glass, leaving the water on top perfectly clear—which represents the light one sees during meditative states.

The Four Dhyanas have various meanings. These meanings can be anything from the stages of intense meditation, to attaining supernatural powers, to the levels of rebirth in the Dhyana Heavens. But since Li Ching-yun clearly states *self-reliant and independent in all things,* it is obvious he is referring to stages of intense meditation, which are (1) a longing for intense concentration; (2) the desire to apply prolonged, intense effort; (3) the intense desire not to lose or leave the state of dhyana achieved; and (4) the intense state of continual dwelling in dhyana. (Dhyana is Ch'an in Chinese and Zen in Japanese.)

Tailbone refers to the very tip of the tailbone.

Grasp the hands firmly means to clench both hands into fists. The clenching of both hands into fists, in effect, gathers the qi. This closing is the apex of this mysterious art and banishes all bad influences.

The rule is to fashion both the right and left hands into fists. Clench them firmly, with the palms facing heaven and the backs, earth. Then place the hands on the upper part of the knees, which will help maintain the body in being upright and centered. Quiet the mind, getting rid of all confused thinking. The primary idea here is to fully concentrate and then retain that presence of mind.

Author's Comments
Grasp the hands firmly (wo ku) has two techniques and varying purposes throughout the text and exercises. Generally, it refers to the technique of closing the fingers into a fist, with the thumb placed along and outside the fingers. The middle finger of each hand presses in on the center of each palm, known as the Dragon cavity (lung ch'iao) on the left hand and the Tiger cavity (hu ch'iao) on the right hand. The backs of the hands are then placed on the thighs or held close to the lower abdomen.

The main reason for grasping the hands firmly is so that heat energy can be generated in the hands more quickly. You can think of this as how a newborn makes a loose fist in order to conserve heat and energy. In this sense, firmly does not mean that you should tense or flex the muscles, but simply hold them securely, as in the grip of a baby. Tensing and flexing of the hand muscles affect the forearm and biceps, thus blocking off circulation of blood and qi. The correct grip here is achieved by lightly pressing the middle fingers in on the Dragon and Tiger cavities. Gradually, you will be able to sense the pulses in the hands and the stimulation of qi in the Yang Arm and Yin Arm meridians (yang wei mo and yin wei mo), which end in these cavities.

The second method for grasping the hands firmly in regard to these exercises is the t'ai chi knot method, which is simply grasping with one hand the thumb of the other hand and then placing the remaining fingers over the fingers of the hand holding the thumb. The palms of the hands are then placed over the area of the lower abdomen. This method is best employed when sitting quietly or when performing the Second Brocade, Shake the Heavenly Pillar.

To *tap the teeth* is to remove the fire from the heart and to collect the spirit within yourself, making cohesion between the body and spirit.

The procedure is to make the upper and lower teeth tap together thirty-six times, but producing only a slight sound. Do not be hurried in performing this; just exhaust the sound of the tap and, most importantly, do so slowly and lightly. If you become too anxious about this, you could injure the spirit. Just exhausting the sound repeatedly is quite sufficient for removing the fire within the heart; it is otherwise without benefit. Pay attention to this.

Author's Comments

To *exhaust the sound of the tap* means to listen attentively until the sound of each tap dissipates completely before beginning the next tap.

See "Shen" in the "Three Treasures" section in Part 1 for more on uniting body and spirit.

It is said that the head is likened to the top of Mount K'un-lun, the highest peak of the Central Mountains, as the head is also the highest point of a person's body.

The procedure is to mutually interlace the fingers of both hands, with the ten fingers of both hands equally and alternately separated. Once they are securely interlaced, grasp the back of the head—this is to *embrace*. The palms are placed directly over the base of the ears, with the thumbs pointing downward. The elbows are bent, forming a triangle, with the elbows in line with the shoulders.

In this position you should inhale and exhale slowly and calmly, with nine complete respirations through the heels, and then pause. Allow the breath to become completely full when inhaling, and completely empty when exhaling. There must be no audible sound produced. If there is, the qi will then disperse. Through intent, this procedure, without question, will gather the qi.

Author's Comments

The head is metaphorically referred to as K'un-lun Shan, the tallest peak in a great mountain range in western China, likely in consideration that the head is the highest point of a person's body.

Breathe nine times without sound through the nose. First, breathe nine times is a phrase found frequently in Taoist yogic texts. Nine is the supreme yang number, so through breathing nine times, the practitioner stimulates the positive qi of yang. In later stages of cultivation, when the qi is actually able to be circulated, the qi is set into nine complete orbits, at the completion of which a drop of elixir of pure spirit (yang shen tan) is deposited into the lower abdomen.

Without sound means that the breath is inaudible externally. However, because the ears are covered by the palms of the hands, the breath is heard to a degree internally.

The breathing must be done *through the nose*, both the inhalation and exhalation. This is done mainly so that the breath will not dry or burn the throat, and also so that the nose can act as a filter, preventing unwanted particles from entering the system. Rarely is inhalation through the mouth called upon in Taoism.

Breathing *through the heels* refers to Chuang-tzu's statement that "a true man breathes through his heels." The allusion is to the sensation of true breath, which feels as if the entire body is breathing and occurs through the proper application of natural breathing.

The Heavenly Drum is the region both to the left and right and back of both ears, the "hearing door" (tsung men). *Beating* is to produce a drumlike sound internally by tapping the fingers on these areas. This beating can bring about good hearing faculties and also prevents the encroachment of external malignant spirits.

The proper method here is to place the two hands directly over the ear openings (erh men). Place the middle fingers on top of the index fingers, then with some force, snap the middle fingers down. It is essential to be certain that a full echo sound is produced within the ears. Tap left and right alternately twenty-four times each. Start with the left and then do the right side, collectively tapping forty-eight times, and then stop.

Author's Comments

The Heavenly Drum is the area of the occiput and the two neck muscles below the base of the skull. This area is also the location of the Jade Pillow cavity. Covering the ears with the palms of the hands and then tapping along the base of the skull produces a peculiar echoing sound internally, very similar to the sound of a small drum. According to the Taoists, producing this sound coordinates and harmonizes the central nervous system.

The ear opening is likened to the Gates of Life. The number twenty-four is contained in the *secret of the hands:* the Limitless (wu chi), the Two Powers (liang yi), the Four Images (szu hsiang), the Eight Diagrams (pa kua), and the Nine Openings (chiu kung). These represent the twenty-four breaths.

Both the left and right ears must be internally sounded twenty-four times. These twenty-four breaths are to be directed thoroughly though the body via the ears, using the Gates of Life as the source of holding the sound: this is the secret of prolonging the years. The sound produced is the ultimate of sounds and purifies the fire (qi).

Author's Comments
The idea here is to flick the middle finger sharply off the index finger and onto the neck muscles just below the base of the skull. Always begin this procedure with the left-hand fingers, which are on the yang hand. Throughout these exercises, you will notice that every procedure begins on the left, or yang, side.

The twenty-four breaths:
  The Limitless represents the emptiness created between the palms and ear openings. *Wu* means "nothingness" or "to be without." *Chi* means "the ultimate" or "the furthest limit." The term thus refers to what is illimitable, an expression of absolute voidness from which all things are produced. The term was first introduced by the Taoist Chou Tun-yi of the Sung dynasty, who used it to describe a mind completely devoid of all worries, thoughts, emotions, and desires.
  The Two Powers is a term denoting the two powers of yin and yang, sun and moon, heaven and earth, male and female, and so on. The sound of the tapping here represents the separation of yin qi and yang qi from wu chi.
  The Four Images are created from the interaction of yin and yang. In regard to the tapping sound, they represent the eyelids lowered, the tongue held against the palate, the hands held firmly, and the anus drawn up.
  The Eight Diagrams, in relation to the tapping sound, are represented by the following cavities: Returning Yin, Gates of Life, Double Pass, Jade Pillow, Hundred Gatherings, Mysterious Pass, Bright Palace, and Field of Elixir.
  The Nine Openings refer to the two eye sockets, two ear canals, two nostrils, the mouth, the urinary tract, and the anus.
  The meaning here is not that there are twenty-four distinct breaths, rather, that in each of the twenty-four taps, there must be the production and stimulation of the qi. With each alternating tapping, the attention is directed to each of these areas. The tapping is performed slowly enough so that in each area the sound can briefly be held onto.
  The secret of the hands here could also be translated as "one's own hand." The Chinese character that is used (which represents *tzu*) means either "one's own" or "secret." However, Li Ching-yun uses the characters representing

an an in connection with this idea, and so the meaning seems to be "the secret of the palms." Also, many Taoist works make reference to the idea that in the right palm is the Tiger cavity (hu ch'iao) and in the left palm, the Dragon cavity (lung ch'iao). When the palms are placed over the ears (with the centers of the palms cupping the ears completely), the Tiger and Dragon cavities are joined with the ear openings, and once joined with the breath, they create the divine internal sound of the Limitless. In more practical terms, this is the sound created by the empty space between the palms and the ear drums—much like the sound one hears when placing a seashell over the ear. Thus, by closing off the external hearing, the practitioner hears only the inner sounds.

Author's Instructions

- Sit cross-legged and close the eyes. Grasp the hands firmly, using either the t'ai chi knot or the Dragon and Tiger fists. Still the thoughts.
- Perform nine cleansing breaths.
- Breathe deeply and naturally twenty-four times.
- Tap the teeth thirty-six times.
- Open the eyes, embrace K'un-lun Shan (the head), and breathe in and out nine times.
- Beat the Heavenly Drum, alternately tapping forty-eight times.

Once you have sat down in a meditative position, and before breathing the initial twenty-four breaths, first perform nine cleansing breaths to clear your lungs. Then breathe in and out through the nostrils only while slowly and deeply expanding and contracting the abdomen twenty-four times. Keep the tongue on the roof of the mouth. It is important to regulate the body posture, making sure the spine is erect and the head is suspended as if by an imaginary string.

When first doing this exercise, be aware and cautious of any subtle strain in the lungs. If you feel any tension, relax and start over again. The correct manner of breathing is to be slow and precise. Afterward, simply be aware of your improved spirits. This method is the best way to strengthen the lungs for long-lasting health and vitality.

With the fists still closed firmly, slowly and precisely tap the teeth together thirty-six times. Keep the head upright and the eyes lowered. Listen intently to the sound of the tapping.

The lower teeth are raised and lowered in relation to the upper teeth in a chewing or grinding manner, just as if eating food, but slowly. Breathe naturally during the tapping motion. This exercise helps the teeth and gums become strong and firm.

With the eyes open and the tongue up against the palate, bring both palms up to cup the ears. Tilt the head back slightly and breathe inaudibly and naturally nine times through the nose.

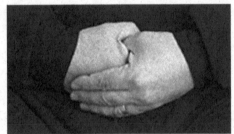

T'ai chi knot

Dragon and Tiger fists

Refrain from applying any force or tension in either tilting the head back or covering the ears. The eyes gaze outward as if looking into empty space. The application of this method can also make the vision more alert and acute.

Covering the ears

Covering the ears, rear view

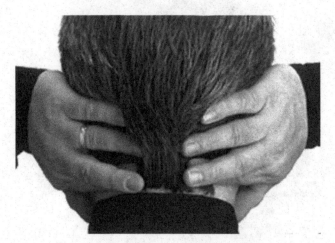

Middle fingers placed over index fingers

Slide both hands back so that the palm butts cover the ear openings. Place the middle fingers over their respective index fingers. Using the middle finger of each hand, snap lightly off the top of the index finger and tap the back of the head, alternately left and right, forty-eight times (twenty-four on each side). Breathe naturally throughout and do not tap too quickly, as it will make the mind anxious.

By striking the occiput region in this manner, you strengthen and stretch the membrane of the inner eardrum, which can promote excellent hearing.

This brocade stimulates the brain.

THE SECOND BROCADE

SHAKE THE HEAVENLY PILLAR

This chapter, like the preceding, begins with my translation of the instructions, commentary, and correct method that were included in the Kao Lin engraving. Following the original text are Li Ching-yun's commentary and my comments, and finally my instructions for practicing the Second Brocade.

The Original Text

Gently shake the Heavenly Pillar.

Sway the head left and right while gazing at the shoulders. Do so alternately in conjunction with the movements, twenty-four times. It is necessary to first grasp the hands firmly.

The correct method: *First, grasp the hands firmly. Alternately turn the head left and right, gazing toward the shoulders when following the movements of the head, twenty-four times.*

Author's Comments

Note the position of the hands and head in the drawing. The hands are not closed into fists; rather, the right hand is placed on top of the left palm, and the head is tilted upward and away from the left shoulder. This is another example of the variant meanings of "grasp the hands firmly."

In this brocade, the hands should be held in the t'ai chi knot. When the practitioner is gazing toward the left side, the right hand grasps the left thumb and the left hand covers the back of the right hand. When the practitioner is gazing to the right side, the positioning is exactly the opposite. (See the photographs.)

For further information, refer to the book *Tibetan Yoga and Secret Doctrines* by W. Y. Evans-Wentz (Oxford University Press, 1975). The Nine Bellowslike Breathing exercise, explained in the section on producing psychic heat, is very similar to this exercise of Shake the Heavenly Pillar.

Li Ching-yun's Commentary

The Heavenly Pillar is the spinal column and the connective neck bone. To *gently shake* (to wave to and fro) means to sway the shoulders. *Gently shake the Heavenly Pillar* means to crick and move the neck. Properly, the neck is cricked to the left and right sides along with a gazing procedure. The two shoulders are followed by the gaze when swaying. The left and right sides are counted separately, with each side being performed twenty-four times, and collectively forty-eight times.

This cricking of the neck, swaying of the shoulders, and gazing in accordance with the movements in effect remove the fire of the heart and eliminate any invasions or disturbances of external malignant spirits.

Author's Comments

The Heavenly Pillar is a Taoist metaphor for the spinal column and connective neck bone. The first character (representing wei) of this section of the text normally translates as "subtly" or "secretly." Following Li Ching-yun's lead, I consider it best to translate this as "gently."

Note that under the "Concluding Exercises" at the end of Part 2, there is also the instruction to shake the shoulders, but that exercise is distinct from this one. I bring this up because many Eight Brocades texts, in both English and Chinese, do not differentiate between these two methods.

Author's Instructions

- Using the t'ai chi knot method, shake the Heavenly Pillar twenty-four times, gazing first to the left twelve times and then to the right twelve times.

With the legs crossed, grasp the hands firmly using the t'ai chi knot (right hand grasping left-hand thumb) and place the bottom edge of the right palm on the right thigh, near the hip, and with the Tiger's Mouth cavity (hu k'o)—the indentation formed at the base of the thumb and index finger—facing upward. Place the tongue against the roof of the mouth.

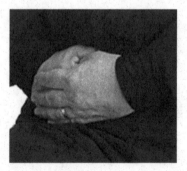

Preparing to shake the Heavenly Pillar toward the left

Begin to gently shake the Heavenly Pillar by turning the right shoulder, spine, and head toward the left. Inhale while turning and direct the eyes to the top of the left shoulder, then continue by gazing up and back as far as possible, stretching and twisting the spine smoothly, gradually, and in conjunction with natural breathing. Simultaneously, the right hand is pressed into the right thigh and the left-hand thumb joint is pressing down on the right-hand Tiger's Mouth cavity. Then exhale and bring the gaze back down to the shoulder and then to the front. Repeat this twelve times.

Eyes gaze upward and to the left

Right hand presses into right thigh

Shaking the Heavenly Pillar toward the left

Next, perform the exercise from the right, or opposite, side: the left hand grasps the right thumb and presses down on the left thigh, while the thumb joint of the right hand presses into the left-hand Tiger's Mouth and the eyes gaze up and over the right shoulder. Again, perform the movements twelve times.

This brocade is good for strengthening the spine, exercising the eyes, and increasing the blood flow to the waist, legs, and hands.

This brocade stimulates the spleen.

Left hand presses into left thigh

Preparing to shake the Heavenly Pillar toward the right

Eyes gaze upward and to the right

Shaking the Heavenly Pillar toward the right

Left hand presses into left thigh

THE THIRD BROCADE

THE RED DRAGON

STIRS THE SEA

Thchapter, following the format of the previous two, begins
with my translation of the instructions, commentary, and correct method
that were included in the Kao Lin engraving. Following the original text are
Li Ching-yun's commentary and my comments, and finally my instructions
for practicing the Third Brocade.

The Original Text

The Red Dragon stirs up the saliva.

The Red Dragon is the tongue, which moves in a circle inside the mouth, teeth, jaws, and the cheeks, first to the right and then to the left. This produces saliva for swallowing.

Rouse and rinse [the mouth with] the saliva thirty-six times.

Until it swells into one mouthful.

Evenly fill the mouth with Divine Water;

Each mouthful is divided into three parts and swallowed.

After rinsing [the mouth with] the saliva, divide it into three equal parts.

Imitate the sound of ku ku when swallowing.

When the dragon moves, the tiger flees.

The saliva represents the dragon and the breath the tiger. Move the tongue left and right along the roof of the mouth thirty-six times. Rinse thirty-six times. Divide the saliva into thirds in the mouth and, just as if it were a solid substance, gulp each portion down. Afterward this procedure will activate the fire.

The correct method: *The tongue stirs about the mouth and teeth, both to the left and right, until the cheeks are full of saliva; rinse and then swallow.*

Author's Comments

Activating the fire is the result of swallowing the saliva. It is through this swallowing that the heat (qi in the lungs, solar plexus, and heart region) is directed downward to the lower abdomen. To do the swallowing properly, you should visualize and sense the saliva as it moves downward.

In all the original texts, the attached illustration to this brocade shows the hands and arms held upward and over the head, with the hands formed into fists. More contemporary texts have eliminated this deportment altogether. The original text itself makes no mention of this other than by illustration. However, other Taoist sources reveal that this deportment not only aids in sinking the qi into the lower abdomen but also raises the shen as well.

Li Ching-yun's Commentary

Red Dragon is a name for the tongue. The tongue is the tool by which the saliva is produced and therefore functions as the source of good health. It is said that a bright red tongue is a sign of good health. Here it functions as the collector and stimulator of saliva.

The correct procedure is to begin by placing the tongue against the inside of the left cheek. Move the tongue from the left cheek in a rolling motion up and over to the right cheek, passing over the front of the upper gums and teeth, and then continue down in front of the lower gums and teeth back up to the left cheek again. Make eighteen complete (clockwise) revolutions of the tongue around the inside of the mouth. Next, with the tongue positioned on the right cheek, make the opposite movements towards the left cheek. Make eighteen complete (counterclockwise) revolutions of the tongue around the inside of the mouth.

If, during this procedure, you should become unsettled or disturbed, you should pause to compose yourself and get rid of any anxiety; otherwise the source of your good health may well become damaged.

Rouse and rinse means to gather the saliva in the mouth. The qi is stimulated during the in and out motions of rinsing. *Thirty-six* is the number of revolutions. This procedure in effect causes the circulation and stimulation of qi so that it can penetrate deeply.

The method is to use the tongue to stir up and produce saliva and to accumulate it into a single batch. Then, press it forward as if to spit it out. When it reaches the tip of the tongue, this is the completion of issuing the saliva; when reaching the base of the tongue, this is the end of withdrawing the saliva. One out (issuing) and one in (withdrawing) is counted as one full cycle. When having completed thirty-six cycles, stop.

Author's Comments
Rinse means to suck the saliva back and forth from the base of the tongue to its tip.

The term *Divine Water* refers to the saliva. With the mouth full of saliva after having performed *rousing and rinsing thirty-six times*, the saliva becomes a uniform mixture and spreads evenly throughout the mouth. At this time, the breath and qi will also be uniformly spread throughout the body.

Author's Comments
The more experienced and proficient you become with this gathering and swallowing of the saliva, the thicker and more substantial the saliva actually becomes, both in consistency and quantity. After a time, it will feel more solid in the mouth and take on a whiter color, rather than the watery, clear quality that is indicative of bad health. As the saliva becomes more substantial and white, so too will the sexual secretions. In Taoism, saliva and sexual secretions are very closely related as health-giving fluids and components of the elixir of immortality.

The *Divine Water* is the saliva. In Taoism, the saliva is also referred to as *jade juice;* Buddhists call it *sweet dew.* Unlike Westerners, who consider saliva an unwanted and useless bodily secretion, the Eastern mystic has, since antiquity, embraced it as both an aid and a medicine for health and spiritual cultivation. However, saliva is divine only if swallowed correctly. To correctly swallow the saliva, the yogin stretches his neck slightly upward and directs the saliva downward, by visualization, into the Function meridian, thus bringing the fire (breath) down into the lower abdomen. After a long period of correct practice, swallowing saliva will cause a vibration and slight sound when the saliva drops into the lower abdomen, creating an internal sound like thunder rumbling off in the distance or like a drop of water falling into an empty bucket. Ingesting the saliva also serves as a preliminary discipline of a higher yogic practice of ingesting qi.

It is said that if you succeed in swallowing the saliva correctly, you are well on the way to immortality.

Each mouthful means the mouthful of saliva. *Three parts and swallowed* means that the mouthful of saliva is divided into three equal parts and swallowed down successively. It is completely unintentional that this is analogous to the Three Powers.

Author's Comments
Ku ku (phonetically "guu guu") is the sound akin to that produced when gargling or when water goes down a drain. The characters also represent a compound meaning the sound of waves.

The Three Powers (san tsai) are the three powers of heaven, earth, and man.

The terms *dragon* and *tiger* are metaphors for yang and yin energy, respectively. There is no truth to the idea that there is actually a dragon or tiger residing in the body. The dragon referred to in *the dragon moves* is the spirit within you; the tiger in *the tiger flees* is the qi within you.

Now, just as when collecting the saliva, rousing and rinsing, mixing and dividing, and swallowing down, the results are a fullness of spirit and qi, harmony of the yin and yang energies, and your entire being united peacefully like heaven and earth.

Author's Comments
When the dragon moves, the tiger flees. This particular line of the text has been entirely deleted by most modern commentators. Why is hard to guess. The dragon and tiger are symbols for many Taoist concepts crucial to understanding these eight exercises. For example, the dragon represents yang, spirit, and water (saliva). The tiger represents yin, breath, and fire. Hence, yang and yin, spirit and energy qi, water and fire, and the saliva and breath are all regulated, balanced, and in harmony with each other. In Eight Diagram philosophy, the dragon is symbolized as k'an (symbol for water) and the tiger as li (fire). In every Taoist work, you'll find pairs such as dragon and tiger, lead and mercury, yin and yang, green and yel-

low, and so on, to describe the idea of fire and water. There are almost as many of these dialectic associations as there are schools of Taoism.

What you must understand about these terms is that they are not meant to be taken literally. The idea in Chinese philosophy concerning the Five Elements (wu hsing: metal, wood, fire, water, and earth) is that each element (hsing) has an activity or quality associated with it.

So, this line of text reveals that, if the saliva (dragon) is stimulated (moved) from above [the mouth] through swallowing, the fire (tiger), as a matter of course, will enter into the lower abdomen (naturally flees). In other words, the breath (qi or fire), which in most people is congested in the lungs, will, by means of swallowing the saliva, be taken into the lower abdomen. On another level, the text is relating that the saliva leads the breath, the yang leads the yin, the shen (spirit) leads the qi (energy), or the dragon leads the tiger.

Author's Instructions

- Close the eyes and grasp the hands firmly using the Dragon and Tiger fists.
- When proficient, perform tortoise breathing with the Four Activities, swallowing the breath nine times with the sound of *ku ku*.
- The Red Dragon stirs up the saliva seventy-two times, rousing first to the left thirty-six times and then to the right; when proficient, add simultaneous eyeball rotation.
- Rinse the saliva for thirty-six cycles.
- Divide the Divine Water into three equal parts, swallowing three times with the sound of *ku ku*. When proficient, combine with the Four Activities.

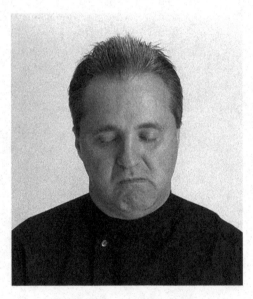

Rousing the saliva to the left

Sitting cross-legged, grasp the hands firmly using the Dragon and Tiger fists. Place the tongue on the roof of the mouth and begin rotating the tongue toward the left cheek, then to the lower jaw, up to the right cheek, and then back to the palate. Circle the tongue smoothly in this manner thirty-six times, first to the left and then thirty-six times to the right. Breathe naturally while circling with the tongue. This is rousing.

When you get the knack of circling with the tongue in this man-

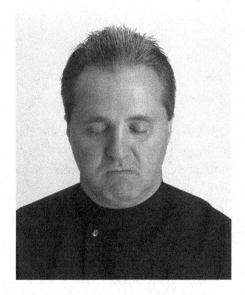

Rousing the saliva to the right

ner, proceed to include simultaneous eyeball rotation as well, with the eyelids closed. When the tongue is on the roof of the mouth, the eyes gaze inward and up; they circle down toward the cheek along with the tongue, gazing downward when the tongue moves to the lower jaw, and so on.

The mouth should now contain a quantity of saliva. Place the tongue against the teeth and begin sucking the saliva back and forth along the length of the tongue. Do so thirty-six times (each back-and-forth motion is one cycle) while maintaining natural breathing. This is rinsing.

With the mouth full of saliva, bring the hands up over the head, holding them in fists with the palms facing front and the elbows slightly bent. Place the tongue against the roof of the mouth, divide off one-third of the saliva, and swallow with a gulping action (making the sound guu guu). When swallowing, stretch the neck up a little and tilt the head back just slightly (this is to ensure the saliva's proper descent down the esophagus and the descent of the qi down the Function meridian channel). Divide off another third of the saliva and again gulp it down in the same manner. Finally, gulp the last third down.

When gulping, listen each time to the "guu guu" sound the gulping creates. This is swallowing.

For true tortoise breathing, before beginning to produce the saliva one should do as instructed in the *Huang ti nei ching*:

> Breathe deeply seven times, each time "stopping the breath"
> qi, extending the neck, and swallowing the breath. As one
> does so, it should be as if one is swallowing something hard.
> Having done this seven times, move the tongue around and
> swallow the saliva produced several times.

It is advised to get the knack of swallowing just saliva first and later adding the swallowing of air. Regardless of whether you are swallowing air or saliva, eventually you should be applying the Four Activities to this exercise. As discussed in the beginning of Part 2, the Four Activities help you to learn how to guide qi through the Lesser Heavenly Circuit, which is explained in Part 3.

For this exercise, apply the Four Activities each time before you swallow. That is, with the fists raised above the head, draw in the anus, roll the eyes upward and back to visualize the Jade Pillow cavity, form the magpie bridge with the tongue, and slowly inhale and stop the breath for twelve heartbeats. While holding the breath, send the qi up from the Returning Yin cavity and into the Hundred Gatherings cavity. After swallowing and exhaling, send the qi down to the lower abdomen.

At first you will have to imagine this process, but eventually, through continuous practice, you will be able to sense the qi move up the back and down the front of the body.

With this exercise the qi and ching are swallowed (sunk) into the lower abdomen.

This brocade stimulates the lungs.

Applying the Four Activities

THE FOURTH BROCADE

RUB THE COURT OF THE KIDNEYS

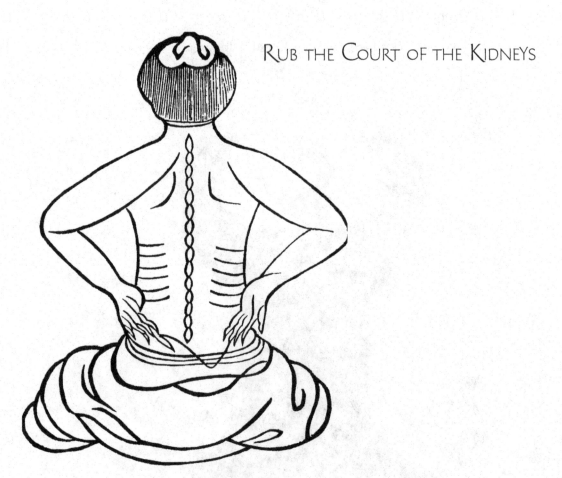

This chapter, as in the preceding, begins with my translation of the instructions, commentary, and correct method that were included in the Kao Lin engraving. Following the original text are Li Ching-yun's commentary and my comments, and finally my instructions for practicing the Fourth Brocade.

The Original Text

Stop the breath and rub the hands until hot;

Breathe in pure air through the nose and then close it off for a short period. Afterward, rub the hands together rapidly numerous times until heat is produced. When this is achieved, let the air exit from the nose slowly.

On the back, massage the court of the kidneys.

The kidneys are on the back side of the waist, outward from the spine. In unison, rub them with the palms. When finished, withdraw the hands and firmly close them into fists.

Entirely exhaust one breath;

Again close off the breath.

Imagine the heat aflame at the Navel Wheel.

The nose and mouth close off the breath. Use the imagination to think the fire down from the heart, like a flame entering the lower abdomen. Be aware of the warmth and, when it becomes extreme, employ the following procedure.

The correct method: *Stop the breath, rub the hands until warm, then rub the area of the kidneys the number of times mentioned. When finished, draw the hands back as before, closing the hands firmly, and again close off the breath. Imagine that the fire of the heart is sent downward into the lower abdomen to heat it. When experiencing extreme warmth, proceed to the next exercise.*

Author's Comments

Court of the kidneys here refers to the area of the kidneys. "Court" is used frequently in connection with the viscera so the practitioner will clearly distinguish between massaging the area (the court) and massaging a specific cavity (in this case, the Gates of Life cavity).

Li Ching-yun's Commentary

Stop the breath means that the internal qi is preserved within and not dissipated externally. *Rub the hands until hot* means, in effect, that the pulses are united during the motions of both hands moving back and forth.

Stopping the breath and rubbing the hands results in the qi being collected and the pulses harmonized. Internal impurities can be driven off and external malignant spirits cannot encroach.

The proper procedure starts in a seated and cross-legged posture, with the two palms placed together. First, with the left hand on top and the right below, circularly rub in a leftward (counterclockwise) motion twenty-four times. Then both palms change positions, with the right on top and the left below. Circularly rub in a rightward (clockwise) motion twenty-four times. This concludes the procedure.

Author's Comments

Closing off or *stopping the breath* the Taoists also call shutting the door of heaven (the nose) and closing the gate of earth (the mouth). *Stopping the breath* aids in directing the qi, in this particular case into the hands. This practice is used throughout the exercises and is highly developed in more esoteric Taoist practices.

On the back massage the Gates of Life means placing the hands on the back and massaging the kidney area. After having previously rubbed the hands together forty-eight times or to the point where the hands become very hot, place the hands securely over the Gates of Life. Perform the massaging motions simultaneously with both the right and left hands. Each hand circles outward and inward, twenty-four times.

Afterward, *close the hands firmly*, just like in the earlier procedure of the same name, and place the back of the hands on the knee areas.

Author's Comments
The Chinese for kidneys, ching men, translates literally as "semen door." Taoists believe that ching (sexual energy or force, whether male or female) is stored in the kidneys. Therefore, to properly stimulate this essence, the kidneys must be stimulated. Some contemporary writers have criticized this idea, taking ching literally as semen and then making a case that Taoists and Chinese physicians in general had no conception of anatomy and biological processes if they believed that semen was stored in the kidneys. Taoists believe that it is the energy of sex—a vital principle, regenerative force, biological sexual energy, and so forth—that resides in the kidneys, not the physical substance of sexual secretions.

The true master of a person is the breath. The explanation given for completely exhausting this one breath is "to exhaust is to accumulate the qi within yourself and is called gathering from within."

To *imagine the heat* means that your own imagination produces the fire; the fire is given imaginary form, but it is not real fire.

To *imagine the heat aflame at the Navel Wheel* means that your imagination perceives that there is a fire burning below in the Navel Wheel region.

When the qi is concentrated, use the mind to concentrate on this fire. Circulate the true yang by fixing the intent downward into the lower abdomen and on the flame.

This, however, is still not the true fire (qi), for men's eyes are incapable of seeing it. Nevertheless, in regard to circulation, the result will be a sustained awareness of warm qi in the lower abdomen as if there were a real fire burning. However, when the lower abdomen is first heated, there will be an overanxious attempt to accumulate more, but this will only cause it to dissipate. It can be restored again by "darkening the heart in a seated posture."

Author's Comments

The center of the *Navel Wheel* (ts'i lun) is the point in the human body where the umbilical cord attaches (the navel). The character used to represent ts'i (for navel) also represents the point at which a corn kernel attaches itself to the husk. This Navel Wheel is distinguished from the lower abdomen in that it encompasses the entire area below the lower abdomen to the pubic bone region and up to the area just below the "bright palace" (ming ku), or the area contained within the qi cavities of Yellow Court (huang ting) and Original Pass (kuan yuan). In kundalini yoga, this Navel Wheel area corresponds to the Manipura chakra.

The spiritual embryo being formed within the Navel Wheel

Author's Instructions

- Keeping the eyes closed, stop the breath and then rub the hands until hot.
- Rub the palms in a circular motion over the kidney area forty-eight times.
- Stop the breath and heat the hands again, then rub the backs of the fists over the kidneys another forty-eight times.
- Entirely exhaust one breath—inhale completely, hold the breath for two heartbeats, and exhale over twelve heartbeats. Imagine the heat aflame at the Navel Wheel.

Heating the hands

Accumulate the qi by putting both palms together tightly and rubbing them vigorously until the palm centers are hot. Always, when stopping the breath, remember to incorporate the Four Activities. Keep the eyes closed while rubbing the kidneys. It is essential that the palms are made hot before rubbing the kidneys.

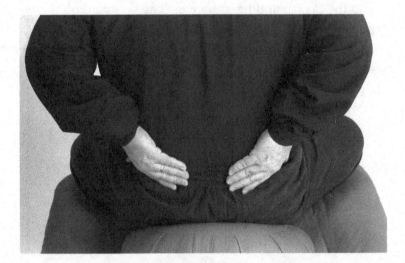

Rubbing the palms over the kidney area

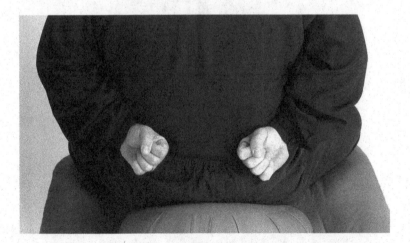

Rubbing the backs of the fists over the kidney area

This brocade stimulates the kidneys.

Move on to the Fifth Brocade, meditate, or perform the Internally Opening the Eight Subtle Qi Cavities regime, or the Lesser Earthly, Human, or Heavenly circuits—depending on how advanced you are in your practice.

Exhausting the breath

THE FIFTH BROCADE

THE SINGLE PASS WINDLASS

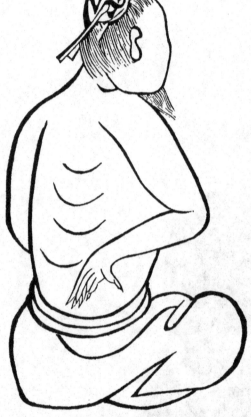

This chapter, as in the preceding, begins with my translation of the instructions, commentary, and correct method that were included in the Kao Lin engraving. Following the original text are Li Ching-yun's commentary and my comments, and finally my instructions for practicing the Fifth Brocade.

The Original Text

Left and right, turn the Windlass.

Bend the head by moving it to and fro toward each shoulder, thirty-six times. Imagine the heat moving up from the lower abdomen into the Double Pass cavity and then into the brain. The nose takes in the pure air and then closes it off for a brief period.

The correct method: *Bend the head as the body moves to and fro. Move the left shoulder thirty-six times and the right shoulder thirty-six times.*

Author's Comments

Note the positioning of the hands in the drawing. The back of the right palm is placed on the back near the kidneys. The left hand, hidden from view, is placed with the palm over the lower abdomen; this is the rightward style. In the leftward style of this brocade, the hands are placed exactly opposite to this.

Other than in the earlier texts, there is no reference made to this deportment, and in many contemporary works it is eliminated altogether. It may be that many later commentators felt that the Fifth and Sixth Brocades were so similar that the fifth one could be eliminated altogether. Li Ching-yun, interestingly enough, comments on only this deportment.

Li Ching-yun's Commentary

To *turn the Windlass* is expressed through the hands, arms, and shoulders. First, bend the left arm and then, in unison with the shoulder, revolve the arm and shoulder leftward thirty-six times. Afterward, the right arm is likewise revolved toward the right thirty-six times. This circling is the method for mobilizing the blood. After a total of seventy-two times on the left and right sides, as before, return to closing the hands firmly and the original seated posture.

Author's Comments

The word for *windlass* has been translated in the past as "pulley," which may or may not have some justification. The Chinese characters used (representing lu lu) and the physical action of this exercise clearly suggest the idea and function of a windlass, an apparatus used in drawing a water bucket from a well. It appears from the instructions that windlass has a twofold meaning. On the one hand, the action of turning a windlass to draw a bucket of water is similar to the gesturing in the Fifth Brocade, the Single Pass Windlass, and that in the Sixth Brocade, the Double Pass Windlass. At the same time, the heat (qi) is being gathered, like filling the bucket with water at the bottom of the well, in the Single Pass Windlass.

In the Double Pass Windlass, the heat qi is drawn upward, like the bucket itself as the windlass is cranked.

To date, I have yet to come across any Eight Brocades materials in English that mention these two original windlass methods, much less make a distinction between them. It seems odd that the contents of the original methods would be so easily ignored.

Author's Instructions

- Wind the Single Pass Windlass seventy-two times—thirty-six times to the left, circling counterclockwise, then thirty-six times to the right, circling clockwise.
- Using the Dragon and Tiger fists, stop the breath for twelve heartbeats.

Place the back of the right wrist and hand firmly on the lower back (kidney area). Place the left-hand palm over the lower abdomen region.

Begin by applying slight pressure on the lower abdomen with the left hand. Maintaining the pressure, circle the hand counterclockwise (first downward and to the left and then upward and to the right). The right wrist and hand are placed on the back near the kidneys and follow the motion of the left hand. Simultaneously rotate the left shoulder up and over to the right side in conjunction with the hand movements. The head is also bent left and right in unison with the hands and shoulders. In the left version of the exercise the head bends toward the left shoulder when the hands descend to the left and toward the right shoulder when the hands move upward toward the right.

When performing the movements to the right, the hands circle in a clockwise fashion and the right shoulder moves up and over to the left side, with the head bending toward the right shoulder when the hands descend to the right, and toward the left shoulder when the hands move upward toward the left.

The left and right versions are performed alternately seventy-two times (thirty-six times on each side). This exercise circulates the blood and qi throughout the entire body.

This brocade stimulates the heart.

Winding the Single Pass Windlass to the left

Winding the Single Pass Windlass to the right

THE SIXTH BROCADE

THE DOUBLE PASS WINDLASS

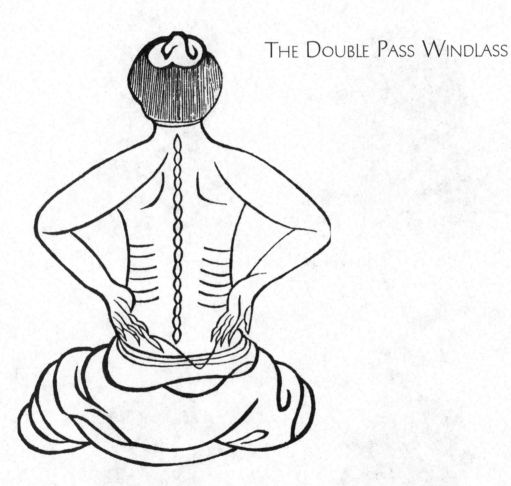

This chapter, as in the preceding, begins with my translation of the instructions, commentary, and correct method that were included in the Kao Lin engraving. Following the original text are Li Ching-yun's commentary and my comments, and finally my instructions for practicing the Sixth Brocade.

The Original Text

Wind the Double Pass Windlass.

Stretch out both feet loosely;

Loosely place both legs out.

The correct method: *The shoulders are moved equally like a
pendulum thirty-six times. Imagine the heat in the lower abdomen
passing upward through the Double Pass
and into the brain. Take in pure air
through the nose. Afterward,
stretch out the legs.*

Author's Comments

Note from the drawing that the hands are open. As with other aspects of Eight Brocades practice, this deportment has been eliminated in contemporary works, and this brocade is usually shown with two fists performing the movement.

The *Double Pass* has two interrelated meanings. The first relates to the two qi channels that intertwine upward and around on the left and right sides of the spinal column. In ancient Taoism, these were referred to as the Blue Dragon and White Tiger. The *Hsing ming chih kuai* (Instructions on the endowments of destiny), a sixth-century Taoist work on meditation and breathing techniques, contains an illustration that clearly explains these two channels.

The second reference is to the Double Pass cavity, which is located on the number one vertebra on the spine. If you were to lean back against a wall, curve your back, and move it up and down, the bone you would feel protruding in the center of your back would be the location of the Double Pass cavity.

The Blue Dragon and White Tiger channels intersect at the Double Pass cavity. It is difficult for the qi to pass through this cavity because the skin and bone here are so closely knit that the blood has difficulty passing through. If blood flow is difficult, the flow of qi will be difficult as well.

Li Ching-yun's Commentary

After having performed each of the previous seated exercises, having endured them for a long period of time, the lower limbs can experience tiredness, and if they are not readjusted, they will certainly become exhausted. For this reason, they should be allowed to stretch out. The method is to simply uncross the folded legs and gradually stretch them out toward the front, straightening them completely.

These exercises should not cause excessive tiredness, but if the legs do become very weary after you have sat cross-legged for a long period of time, they must be stretched out. Otherwise, the result will be that the veins and arteries of the lower limbs could possibly suffer some sort of injury.

Author's Comments

Li's commentary immediately above would normally follow after his comments in the Fifth Brocade. However, because I have chosen to explain both the Single Pass Windlass and the Double Pass Windlass deportments—which is in keeping with the original text—I have placed his comments here, at the end of the Sixth Brocade.

Author's Instructions

- Wind the Double Pass Windlass alternately thirty-six times.
- Grasp the hands firmly and breathe naturally twenty-four times.
- Stretch the legs out loosely.

Both hands are held open with the back of the wrists placed on the waist. The eyes gaze straight ahead. Sway the shoulders like a pendulum, twisting the torso to move the left shoulder first, then the right, alternately thirty-six times, as though rowing a boat with first the left oar and then the right.

This brocade stimulates the liver.

Back of the wrists placed on the waist

*Winding the Double Pass Windlass
to the left*

*Winding the Double Pass Windlass
to the right*

Stretching the legs out

THE SEVENTH BROCADE

SUPPORTING HEAVEN

This chapter, as in the preceding, begins with my translation of the instructions, commentary, and correct method that were included in the Kao Lin engraving. Following the original text are Li Ching-yun's commentary interspersed with my comments, and finally my instructions for practicing the Seventh Brocade.

The Original Text

Afterward both hands support the Void.

> The fingers of both hands interlace and are turned upward to
> support the Void, three or nine times.
>
> **The correct method:** Rub the two hands together, then make
> five voluntary coughs. Both hands are mutually interlaced
> and raised upward to support
> the Void.

Li Ching-yun's Commentary

Both hands means that the fingers are mutually interlaced, so that all ten fingers are equally separated.

To *support the Void* means, even though the hands do not really raise anything substantial upward, you imagine as you raise them upward that the emptiness above is being supported.

The correct procedure is to interlace both hands at the level of the chest, with the backs of the hands facing heaven. Turn the palms face up when raising them. Make use of some imaginary resistance in supporting the Void. The backs of the hands should be directly over the topmost gate (the Hundred Gatherings cavity). After having raised both arms completely, gradually lower them. Each movement, upward and downward, is counted as one time. Perform these actions nine times. Then, as before, close the hands firmly and place them on top of the area of the knees.

Author's Comments

Support the Void refers to the title of the Seventh Brocade, Supporting Heaven, which implies the action of pushing or pressing upward against something. Here it can be thought of as supporting something above the head. In practice, you should imagine lifting something over your head by first pressing (as if there were a resistance or weight) upward and then holding it there.

Three and nine are the "supreme yang" numbers. Nine is the triple yang number.

The *voluntary coughs* are like the sound of a half cough, as when clearing your throat, *ahem*.

Author's Instructions

- With the legs either stretched out in front or in a cross-legged position, stop the breath and rub the hands together until hot. Press the hands tightly together and make five half coughs.
- Support the Void nine times, stopping the breath for twelve heartbeats or more while the arms are outstretched.

Interlace the fingers of the hands so that the palms can be turned out and raised upward. To begin, the fingers should be interlaced securely, with the palms facing the chest. Keep your eyes focused on your hands.

Next, inhale and stretch the hands upward to the furthest extent, simultaneously turning the palms to face out and upward, as if pushing something up and then supporting it. Then hold the breath for twelve heartbeats, incorporating the Four Activities. When bringing the hands downward, exhale while loosening the grip and returning the hands to face the chest again. Allow the hands to be naturally loose while facing the chest.

At this point, you may inhale and exhale again to restore your breath before inhaling, supporting the Void, and stopping the breath again. Repeat this process of supporting the Void a total of nine times.

This brocade stimulates the spine.

Interlacing the fingers

Supporting the Void

THE EIGHTH BROCADE

GRASPING WITH HOOKS

This chapter, as in the preceding chapters, begins with my translation of the instructions, commentary, and correct method that were included in the Kao Lin engraving. Following the original text are Li Ching-yun's commentary interspersed with my comments, and finally my instructions for practicing the Eighth Brocade.

The Original Text

Repeatedly bend the head over and seize the feet.

The two hands are made into hooks. Move them forward and grasp the soles of the feet twelve times.

The correct method: *Both hands are moved forward to grasp the soles of each foot twelve times and then they are withdrawn so to sit upright.*

Li Ching-yun's Commentary

This is the method for unifying the sinews and arteries of the whole body. This so-called *bending the head over* means it is not enough to just bend the cranium forward, but the entire upper torso must equally be bent forward and down.

Begin by separating the fingers of the hands, extending both arms to the front with the palms facing one another. Gradually bend the torso downward. Both hands follow down along the sides of the legs while simultaneously drawing the feet back and inward, then seize the bottoms of the feet (Bubbling Well cavities). Pause momentarily.

Next, using the head and tailbone in conjunction, slowly unfold and rise into an upright position, finishing with the spine completely straight.

One bowing motion and one rising action constitute one gesture. Perform this gesture a total of twelve times and then rest momentarily.

Author's Comments

Many people have mistranslated this brocade as "grasp the hooks." But, more precisely, it is grasping *with* hooks, as the hands act as the hooks, not the feet.

Both hands are moved forward means the hands press into the sides of the legs as they move down the legs. In addition, the hands make slight back-and-forth motions, as though they were sawing while making their downward progress. This is to stimulate blood circulation in the legs after sitting cross-legged and to activate the qi in the Yang Leg (yang chiao mo) and Yin Leg (yin chiao mo) meridians. *Seize the bottoms of the feet* refers to the activity of pressing in with the thumbs on the Bubbling Well cavities, the hollow space on each foot an inch or so up from the center of the sole (the acupuncture point Kidney 1). The entire process is completed twelve times.

Author's Instructions

- Massage downward along the outer part of the legs, stop the breath, and perform Grasping with Hooks. Grasp for four heartbeats, then release, grasp for another four heartbeats, release, and then grasp a final time for four heartbeats, holding the breath for a total of twelve beats. Repeat this procedure twelve times in all.
- Massage the Bubbling Well cavities with the thumbs in a circular fashion forty-nine times.
- Bend and cross the legs and perform twenty-four natural breaths.

With the legs bent, knees splayed, and soles facing each other, massage down along the outer part of the legs by pressing firmly with the palm butt of both hands, bending over slowly until reaching the feet.

Massaging down along the outer part of the legs

Grasp the feet by wrapping the hands over the upper edge of both feet, the fingers covering the top of the feet and the thumbs pressing in on the center of the soles, the Bubbling Well cavities. Press the thumbs into the soles three times, each time the feet are grasped. The massaging of the legs should be done slowly and naturally.

Inhale before massaging down the legs, then exhale while massaging. Hold the breath when pressing the Bubbling Well cavities. While holding the breath, press in with the thumbs for four heartbeats,

Grasping the feet

then relieve the pressure while still holding the breath and keeping the thumbs on the feet. Then press in again for another four heartbeats, and repeat a third time for a final four heartbeats. In pressing in with the thumbs three times, you will have stopped the breath for a total of twelve heartbeats.

Then exhale and inhale to regulate the breath.

Rise up slowly while exhaling, letting the spine ascend vertebra by vertebra. Keep the hands attached to the legs while rising. The hands should remain touching the legs throughout this exercise.

Perform Grasping with Hooks in the above manner twelve times while breathing naturally.

Afterward, vigorously massage the Bubbling Well cavities with the thumbs in a circular fashion forty-nine times. Cross the legs again and perform twenty-four natural breaths.

These exercises will make the bones and joints of the spine nimble and lively, as well as strengthen the kidneys.

This brocade strengthens the four limbs.

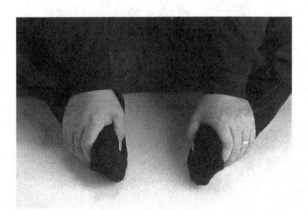

Thumbs pressing into the Bubbling Well cavities

Performing twenty-four natural breaths

CONCLUDING EXERCISES AND COMMENTS

The Kao Lin engraving includes a series of exercises, with comments, intended as a conclusion to the Eight Brocades. This chapter begins with my translation of the instructions, commentary, and correct method as set out in the original Kao Lin text of the concluding exercises. Following my translation of the original text are Li Ching-yun's commentary, interspersed with my explanations, and instructions for performing the concluding exercises. Li Ching-yun's concluding comments appear at the end of this chapter.

Concluding Exercises:
The Original Text

Wait for the water to be produced.

> *Wait for the saliva to be produced in the mouth, without working for it. Again, rapidly stir it up to obtain the water as in the previous procedure.*

Rinse and swallow, dividing it into three parts; altogether swallow the Divine Water nine times.

> *Again rinse thirty-six times just like in the previous instructions. Divide it in the mouth into thirds and swallow, nine times in all.*

Swallow it down with the sound of ku ku;

Then the hundred pulses will be naturally harmonized.

Complete the motion of the River Cart.

> *Shake the shoulders and body twenty-four times and again turn the Windlass twenty-four times.*

Direct the fire to circulate and heat the entire body.

> *Imagine the fire down into the lower abdomen and circulate it upward to heat the entire body. While you are imagining this, the nose and mouth must close off the breath for a short period.*

The purpose of these exercises is to prevent harmful influences from approaching, to provide clearness during sleep and in dreams, to prevent cold and heat from entering, and to keep illness and disease from encroaching.

These exercises should be practiced after Tzu and before Wu. This will create harmony between Ch'ien and K'un, which are connected together by a cyclic arrangement.

Hence, everything connected to [the procedures of] restoring one's original nature and returning to the Tao has excellent reasoning.

The correct method: Produce the saliva within the mouth, again rinse and again swallow once [in three gulps], the number of times previously indicated. Shake the shoulders and body together thirty-six times. Repeat the Windlass twenty-four times. Imagine the heat in the lower abdomen moving upward and downward, so that the entire body is heated. At the time of imagining this, the nose and mouth must close off the breath for a short period.

金
火
土

Li Ching-yun's Commentary

Just as in the previous method of *the Red Dragon stirs up the saliva,* use the tongue to excite and stir up the saliva, until the mouth is full. Accumulate the saliva and then repeat the method of rousing and rinsing and swallowing it down.

The meaning of one time is to rouse and rinse thirty-six times each, then swallow the saliva in three parts. Repeat this process three times, rousing and rinsing one hundred and eight times total and swallowing nine times total.

In performing the previous method three times, swallowing the Divine Water nine times symbolizes the Four Seasons and the Five Activities; this is the reason for the number nine.

Author's Comments
The *four seasons* refers to spring, summer, autumn, and winter; the *Five Activities* are those associated with the elements of metal, wood, fire, water, and earth.

By what means can the saliva produce a divine sound? Through the rousing of the qi. Just as water by itself cannot of its own accord make waves, and needs the wind to do so, at the time of swallowing the saliva, you must make the sound of *ku ku.* Why? Because, through the rousing of the saliva and making this sound, the shen and qi will influence the saliva. Likewise the shen and qi will be brought to fullness. From the ears above, to the lower abdomen below, and throughout all in between, the shen and qi will circulate everywhere and the mind itself will likewise settle.

The source of the hundred pulses is in the blood and qi, of which the shen is the true master. For if the shen is not tranquil, the blood and qi will most certainly be injured. If the blood and qi are injured, the hundred pulses cannot be harmonized. If the hundred pulses are not harmonized, the entire body is weakened and death awaits in secret ambush.

If you are able to perform the previous methods correctly, the shen and qi will then circulate throughout the entire body. The blood will naturally follow and circulate without obstruction. The hundred bones will also acquire good health if the hundred pulses are naturally harmonized. And so we see the wisdom of the phrase *then the one hundred pulses will be naturally harmonized.*

Author's Comments
One hundred pulses is a reference to all the pulses in the body, from the arterioles to the venules and capillaries.

The meaning of *the River Cart* is that, in Taoism, you seek the refinement of true mercury; true mercury is a representation of water. Hence, this explanation gives a more subtle meaning to the term Divine Water.

The meaning of *the motion of* is, in application, like that of drifting with the current in a rowboat.

Each of the previous methods, *rouse and rinse* and *swallowing the saliva,* are the initial catalysts for this method. The importance, then, of the expressions *excite the saliva, rouse and rinse,* and *swallow the saliva* comes from the fact that, afterward, the ching, qi, and shen will be stimulated and moved throughout the entire body and through each of the hundred pulses, thereby completely restoring the primal qi (yuan qi), stabilizing the mind (hsin ting), and calming the spirit (shen ning).

The term *complete* means that the shen and qi are directed to circulate one complete orbit (chou t'ien).

Author's Comments
River Cart is a Taoist expression for rousing, rinsing, and swallowing the saliva and completing the Lesser Heavenly Circuit. *True mercury* is an expression for refined saliva, which is also called "Divine Water."

Shake the shoulders refers to a method of grasping the opposite shoulders with the hands and shaking the body gently in order to invigorate it. This shaking is not taken from the Shake the Heavenly Pillar brocade; rather it entails simply grasping each shoulder with the palm of the opposite hand. Gently shake the body by twisting the waist slightly to the right and the left alternately. (See photo on page 124.)

As mentioned previously, ching, qi, and shen are the Three Treasures: ching is regenerative energy, the very essence of which underlies all sexual forces; qi is breath and vital energy, the essence that allows animation of all existence; and shen is spirit and mind energy, whose essence creates instincts and behavior.

The *fire* is only an imaginary fire, void of any external appearance, and the internal fire is likewise formless; it is the true fire of pure yang (chung yang chen huo).

To *heat the body* means that the true fire of pure yang penetrates entirely into each region of the body, which is brought about through the disciplining of your senses. This is a matter of directing the imagination within, in order that the true fire of pure yang can be produced to naturally heat the body. This is called "forgetting your own form" (wang hsing).

My master once told me long ago that "learning the Tao does not lie in just making the body hot. But if we can speak of the imagination heating the body, then we can get to what is called 'forgetting your own form.'"

There are heterodox schools of thought that have the false view of simply heating the body and so do not practice correctly. Therefore, I purposely present this correct view to all those of the various other schools, so that this secret doctrine will not be misinterpreted and cause them to enter upon a divergent path.

Author's Comments

The heat is directed from the heart down into the lower abdomen, then up the spine into the head, then down again into the lower abdomen. Making the body hot is just a matter of stimulating the qi, not of refining the ching or shen. Li here is trying to say that false teachers just talk of heating the body through breathing and other external means. But real skill comes from being able to do so purely from the mind (either the imagination, the will, or mind-intention). When the mind is able to will the qi to move through the body or create heat, then the shen (spirit) is genuinely strong and can be used to enter higher states of meditation as well.

Forgetting your own form is a difficult experience to explain. In Ch'an Buddhist meditation practice, there is a koan that asks, "What did I look like before my parents were born?" This question really cannot be answered, but it does bring meditators to a completely void and inexpressible state of mind in which they are faced with a great doubt about their very existence. It is here that there can be a *forgetting of one's original form.*

The term *harmful influences* does not necessarily mean hobgoblins and sprites, because first of all there is a saying, "the lot of all the mortals in your environment are quite sufficient enough to injure your body and mind." We merely call all of these harmful influences or malignant spirits. However, if you are able to discipline yourself according to the above procedures, they will surely result in a natural way of warding off harmful influences.

Dreams are a constant cycle of false thinking, which is more than adequate in regard to confusing your spirit. But if you were to learn to control your mind, dreams would naturally vanish, making the spirit free of all confusion.

Cold and heat are external influences. In people, heat usually results in perspiration, and cold in shaking. If these occur, it means that external influences have not yet been done away with and you have yet to discipline yourself. Through discipline, over a long period of time, with these exercises, the body will become stronger and more energetic. The mind will become peaceful and the spirit tranquil, the internal harmful influences will be driven off, and the external influences cannot affect you—all with the result that cold and heat will be incapable of having any influence on you.

Illness and disease comes from the arising of internal impurities, whereby external harmful influences then appear. The true source of these is in the mind and they are caused by the deep influences of the external senses, namely the Seven Passions and Six Desires. It is because of these that disease can arise. Sickness also arises through internal tensions and anxieties created by the passions and the desires of the stomach and mouth, which are bound by a craving for satisfaction; they also bring about illness.

But all types of illness begin with and depend upon the individual. Supposing these exercises are practiced for a long time, then all the muscles will be unaffected by cold and heat. However, if lust for gain and profit still exists, then the result will be disease—all because of improper living habits.

Author's Comments

The *Seven Passions* are joy, anger, sorrow, fear, love, hate, and lust. The *Six Desires* are those things desired through the sense organs of the eyes, ears, nose, tongue, body, and mind.

To prevent harmful influences from approaching, to provide clearness during sleep and in dreams, to prevent cold and heat from entering, and *to prevent illness and disease from encroaching* are commonly referred to as the Four Eradications and are meant to be associated with the Four Increases. Together, they become the Eight Accomplishments, as listed below. See also Li Ching-yun's Introduction to the Eight Brocades in Part 2, which lists eight physical benefits of Eight Brocades practice.

- eradication of all evil influences (you will not be adversely affected by nonpractitioners of the Way)
- eradication of dream states (your spirit will no longer be disturbed)
- eradication of the experience of cold and heat (your body will no longer be confused)
- eradication of all disease (your internal organs will not be confused)
- increased perception (in both your physical and your spiritual environments)
- increased health (greater physical and mental energy and blood circulation)
- increased lightness of the body (greater spirit of vitality)
- increased endurance (mental and physical stamina)

When Tzu passes, yang arises; when Wu passes, yin arises. After midnight and before noon— these are the proper times for the intercourse between yin and yang, because at these times you can begin to clearly distinguish between the pure and the turbid.

The practice of these exercises should be done at these times, for it should be considered as though resembling very intimate friends enjoining. Accordingly, when the qi and shen intertwine within yourself, it is then easy to obtain the function of the Tao.

Ch'ien and K'un are the images of Heaven and Earth. In the beginning, these two cosmic forces, yin and yang, were separate. This is why it is said, "after midnight and before noon," as these are the best times for practicing these exercises. Creating a harmony between Heaven and Earth is the principle for engaging peace, and these time periods are the superior times for bringing harmony between the body and mind.

Connected together means to go full circle and return to the original position. *Cyclic arrangement* refers to the idea of something that is chronological and without interruption. This is what is said of men who practice these exercises according to "after midnight and before noon." Moreover, after a time, join the exercises together so that every day you connect them to complete six rounds. The mind will then become ruler of the body, calm and composed.

Restoring and returning are referring to the Three Restorations (san huan) and Nine Revolutions (chiu fan). In Taoism, the subtleties of the Tao are in the refinement of the elixir, and in Buddhism, in youthfulness and long life.

Author's Comments
The Three Restorations are the ching, qi, and shen. *The Nine Revolutions* are the process of circulating the qi nine times in order to deposit a drop of pure spirit (yang shen) in the lower abdomen.

All the myriad things have an effect, but first they must have a cause. Acquiring a good effect comes from having a good cause; a bad cause brings about a bad result. This is the principle of *a cyclic arrangement,* which is an expression of righteousness. Therefore, diligent practice of these exercises will bring about youthfulness and long life, and the way to immortality; youthfulness and long life come about from this *cyclic arrangement.*

Excellent reasoning indicates that these exercises are an excellent and substantial manner in which to approach the practice of the Tao. How did other masters awaken to the Tao? What was their initial method? These are questions that I asked myself in the beginning. The Tao of strengthening the body is the origin of long life. Even though I do not consider myself an immortal, I have lived for nearly 250 years and have not experienced the ill effects of old age, disease, nor death because I adhered to the practice of these exercises.

Author's Instructions

- Repeat the Third Brocade—one or three times in succession.
- Shake the shoulders thirty-six times.
- Wind the Double Pass Windlass twenty-four times.
- Stop the breath and imagine the qi moving upward to complete the Lesser Heavenly Circuit nine times.
- Conclude with the Restoring Youthfulness practice: hold the breath while you rub the hands together to heat them; then cup them over the face, breathing nine times. Heat the hands again and lightly rub the face thirty-six times.

Shaking the shoulders

When you have completed the Eighth Brocade, you can regard the practice as finished. However, usually in the texts we find that the Third Brocade, the

Red Dragon Stirs the Sea, is repeated. After this, shake the shoulders is performed (see photo) thirty-six times, and then Wind the Double Pass Windlass is performed twenty-four times. Last, stop the breath and imagine the qi moving upward to complete the Lesser Heavenly Circuit nine times.

No matter where you end the exercises, and even if you are only meditating, you should always perform the Restoring Youthfulness exercise. Rub both hands together until hot and then cup the palms over the face and breathe

Restoring Youthfulness practice

naturally. Again rub the hands until hot and massage the face lightly and in a circular motion thirty-six times. With constant practice of this method, the face will naturally redden and shine like that of a young person; wrinkles and cracks in the skin will be removed. It is also good to repeat this procedure before going to bed at night.

Li Ching-yun's Concluding Comments

These exercises should be practiced at the late hour, third watch [11 P.M. to 1 A.M.], and in the early hour, first watch [11 A.M. to 1 P.M.]. This will create harmony between Ch'ien and K'un, which follow a cyclic arrangement, namely the Eight Diagrams, which have excellent reasoning for their arrangements.

Author's Comments
The early Taoists divided the day into twelve two-hour periods. Tzu (11 P.M. to 1 A.M.) is the period when yin energy begins waning and yang energy begins waxing. Wu (11 A.M. to 1 P.M.) is the time when the yang energy begins waning and yin begins waxing. These two time periods are considered the most auspicious times for practice.

Ch'ien and K'un are the primary symbols of the I Ching (Book of Changes). Ch'ien ☰☰ symbolizes Heaven, K'un ☷ , Earth. Ch'ien is comprised of purely yang forces (symbolized by three solid lines) and K'un, of all yin forces (three broken lines), and they are thus complete opposites. Tzu and Wu are the hours when Ch'ien and K'un are most harmonious with each other. There are eight symbols in all, with Ch'ien and K'un occupying the extreme poles. The remaining six images are created through the arrangement of yin and yang lines. All sixty-four images of the I Ching are based on and derived from the Eight Diagrams, which, when multiplied by themselves, equal sixty-four images.

The secret of this method lies in Chia [first of the Ten Heavenly Stems] and in Tzu [first of the Twelve Branches], both of which are during the day and at night, halfway into the hour.

Author's Comments
Chia is the first of the Ten Heavenly Stems and *Tzu* is the first of the Twelve Earthly Branches. It is through the combining of these Ten Heavenly Stems and Twelve Earthly Branches, in chronological order, that the sexagenary cycle (a cycle of sixty years) is created.

Chia and *Tzu* can also be thought of as midnight and noon.

When first commencing with these exercises, the breath must not be let out the mouth; only release the pure air gradually out the nose.

Each day at midnight and noon perform all the exercises at least one time or, if possible, perform them three times in succession. Each time it will bring about greater awareness, alleviate disease, and give an increased sense of lightness of body and the ability to undergo suffering. For it is through toil, not laxness, that immortality comes close at hand!

The exalted masters of days past first named these methods the Eight Brocades. Since then the ancient sages have transmitted them down through the ages. Subsequently, these ancient sages correlated the arrangement of the Eight Diagrams (pa kua, the eight basic images of the I Ching) with the Eight Brocades. Each of the Eight Diagrams has a fixed position (direction) and two distinct meanings (Before Heaven and After Heaven arrangements) attached to it. Why have so many practitioners failed to investigate this correlation between the Eight diagrams and the Eight Brocades?

Author's Comments

There are two arrangements of the pa kua images. The first arrangement was created by the mythical sage-ruler Fu Hsi. The second arrangement belongs to King Wen. Fu Hsi's Before Heaven arrangement of the Eight Diagrams is a reflection of the macrocosmic order of the universe, whereas King Wen's After Heaven arrangement of the Eight Diagrams is meant to put the Before Heaven arrangement into a more earthly perspective. For example, Fu Hsi places Heaven (Ch'ien) in the southernly position. King Wen places Fire (Li) in this position, because Heaven is revealed on Earth by brilliant light, luminous things, and radiance—all of which are aspects of Fire (Li).

The Fu Hsi arrangement is what the I Ching is based on and represents all phenomena (the ten-thousand things, or wan wu). The King Wen arrangement is based on the earthly reflection of each of the eight images of Fu Hsi and represents all numinous aspects.

Purposely close the eyes to see your own eyes; darken the heart to see your own heart.

When first sitting down in a cross-legged manner, slightly extend the back of the left foot at the heel and place firmly against the perineum; this will prevent the ching from leaking out from this cavity.

Author's Comments

Placing the foot against the perineum refers to the Mortal Gate cavity (sheng szu ch'iao). By placing pressure on this cavity with the heel of the left foot, the practitioner can avoid unwanted stirring of the sexual organs during meditation, which, if it occurs, will cause dissipation of the ching gained through meditation practice. It will likewise cause the mind and spirit to be disturbed, scattered, and confused.

This Mortal Gate cavity, the perineum, must be given special attention during the beginning stages of meditation practice. One of the most difficult tasks of a practitioner's development and training is removing the energy blocks and tensions stored in this area. The Taoist immortal Chang San-feng claimed that, when he finally circulated the qi in this region through the repetition of the t'ai chi ch'uan posture Step Back to Chase the Monkey Away, he was able to attain immortality. This is also reputed to be the chief reason why the cross-legged seated posture is so conducive to attaining enlightenment and propagated by almost all traditions of spiritual cultivation—because the spreading of the legs aids in removing and opening the energy obstacles in this area. Much like in physical birth, spiritual birth requires the legs to be open.

Many generations have asked, when hearing of these exercises, Why must they be performed at noon and midnight? However, supposing that your day is leisurely and the mind is tranquil, then you can practice at any time. Whether practicing a little or a lot is a matter of personal discretion. But, if one is busy with work, what then is the best time? You can be confident with the two hours of Chia and Tzu. Those of the Way cannot but understand this!

Appendix to Part 2

Summary of Instructions

The Heavenly Drum

- Sit cross-legged and close the eyes. Grasp the hands firmly, using either the t'ai chi knot or the Dragon and Tiger fists. Still the thoughts.

- Perform nine cleansing breaths.

- Breathe deeply and naturally twenty-four times.

- Tap the teeth thirty-six times.

- Open the eyes, embrace K'un-lun Shan, and breathe in and out nine times.

- Beat the Heavenly Drum, alternately tapping forty-eight times.

Shake the Heavenly Pillar

- Using the t'ai chi knot, shake the Heavenly Pillar twenty-four times, gazing first to the left twelve times and then to the right twelve times.

The Red Dragon Stirs the Sea

- Close the eyes and grasp the hands firmly using the Dragon and Tiger fists.

- Perform tortoise breathing with the Four Activities, swallowing the breath nine times with the sound of *ku ku*.

- The Red Dragon stirs up the saliva seventy-two times, rousing first to the left thirty-six times and then to the right.
- Rinse the saliva for thirty-six cycles.
- Divide the Divine Water into three equal parts, swallowing three times with the sound of *ku ku*. When proficient, combine with the Four Activities.

Rub the Court of the Kidneys

- Keeping the eyes closed, stop the breath and then rub the hands until hot.
- Rub the palms in a circular motion over the kidney area forty-eight times.
- Stop the breath and heat the hands again, then rub the backs of the fists over the kidneys another forty-eight times.
- Entirely exhaust one breath—stopping the breath for two heart-beats and exhaling over twelve heartbeats. Imagine the heat aflame at the Navel Wheel.

The Single Pass Windlass

- Wind the Single Pass Windlass seventy-two times—thirty-six times to the left (counterclockwise), then thirty-six times to the right (clockwise).
- Using the Dragon and Tiger fists, stop the breath for twelve heartbeats.

The Double Pass Windlass

- Wind the Double Pass Windlass alternately thirty-six times.
- Grasp the hands firmly and breathe naturally twenty-four times.
- Stretch the legs out loosely.

Supporting Heaven

- With the legs either stretched out in front or in a cross-legged position, stop the breath and rub the hands together until hot. Press the hands tightly together and make five half coughs.

- Support the Void nine times, stopping the breath for twelve heartbeats or more while the arms are outstretched.

Grasping with Hooks

- Massage downward along the outer part of the legs, stop the breath, and perform Grasping with Hooks. Grasp for four heartbeats, then release, grasp for another four heartbeats, release, and then grasp a final time for four heartbeats, holding the breath for a total of twelve beats. Repeat this procedure twelve times in all.

- Massage the Bubbling Well cavities with the thumbs in a circular fashion forty-nine times.

- Cross the legs and perform twenty-four natural breaths.

Concluding Exercises

- Repeat the Third Brocade—one or three times in succession.

- Shake the shoulders thirty-six times.

- Wind the Double Pass Windlass twenty-four times.

- Stop the breath and imagine the qi moving upward to complete the Lesser Heavenly Circuit nine times.

- Conclude with the Restoring Youthfulness practice: hold the breath while you rub the hands together to heat them; then cup them over the face, breathing nine times. Heat the hands again and lightly rub the face thirty-six times.

The Lesser Heavenly Circuit– The Spiritual Practice

Three Interrelated Techniques

Author's Introduction to the Lesser Heavenly Circuit

Part 3 contains a compilation of several Taoist texts that explain supplementary regimes of the Eight Brocades. Even though the tenets may vary, the main purpose is the same—the circulation of qi through the Lesser Heavenly Circuit. Each regime can be practiced on its own, within the Eight Brocades practice, or in conjunction with others. However, the first regime, Externally Patting the Eight Subtle Meridians and Twelve Cavities, is usually considered a preparation for the Eight Brocades practice. The second regime, Internally Opening the Eight Subtle Qi Cavities, is usually performed between the Fourth and Fifth brocades. The third regime, the actual yogic exercise of the Lesser Heavenly Circuit, can be performed by itself, during the Eight Brocades, or in conjunction with the above regimes.

Development of the Lesser Heavenly Circuit

In many Taoist works, you will find frequent references to the Lesser Heavenly Circuit, or more popularly, the Microcosmic Orbit (hsiao chou t'ien). The Lesser Heavenly Circuit is the term for the process of intentionally circulating qi through the Control and Function meridians. In this process, qi is directed up the spine over the head and down the front of the body to the lower abdomen. Since qi is both energy and breath, if the breath cannot be mobilized, the qi cannot be moved; and if the qi is not mobilized, the blood will not circulate properly. All three (breath, energy, and blood) are interdependent, and they must function as a unit.

The Chinese refer to mobilizing qi as yun qi (transporting qi). If this term is not used or discussed in a Chinese text, the book is considered naive or worthless. Similarly, too many people just read popular English Taoist books and believe that all they need do is visualize qi and that somehow it will magically appear. (Some authors are also guilty of this belief.) To actually *feel*, let alone *move*, qi, you must cultivate it through the regulation and transportation of the breath.

The process, or practice, of the Lesser Heavenly Circuit did not come into use until sometime around the period of the Sui and T'ang dynasties (605 A.D.–905 A.D.). As in the development of the Eight Brocades, it grew out of many other practices that came before it.

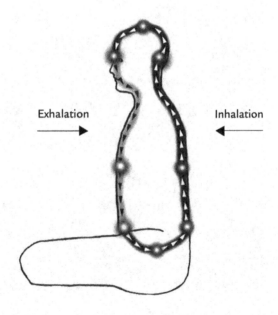

Exhalation

Inhalation

The Lesser Heavenly Circuit

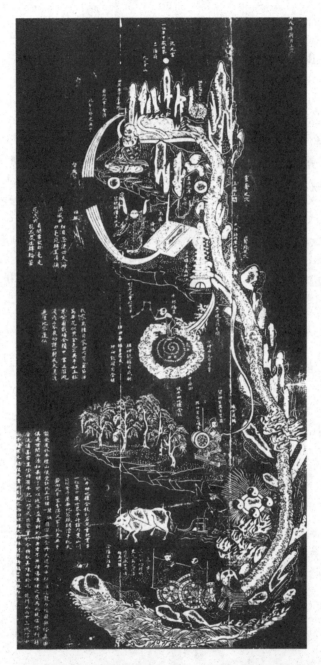

Stone rubbing (completed in 1886 A.D.) of a diagram of the inner alchemical realm of spirits in the body. Taken from the Nei ching tu (Classic on the illustrations of the internal functions). One of the more elaborate versions of the Taoist view of the Lesser Heavenly Circuit, it shows influences of the Mao Shan sect. Original is in White Cloud Monastery, Beijing.

The original arts of nourishing life exercises (sometimes referred to as breath-control exercises) were meant only to restore, strengthen, and purify the Three Treasures, so that the elixir of immortality could be produced. The method of stopping the breath, also called embryonic breathing (t'ai hsi), led the way toward the Lesser Heavenly practice of mobilizing the qi. This type of breathing is very much like Tumo (heat yoga) of Tibetan Buddhism and some *pranayama* regimes of Indian yoga.

In the *Pao-p'u-tzu*, Ko Hung describes an even older method of breathing handed down from the Han dynasty.

> When first practicing mobilizing the breath, inhale through the nose and stop the breath. Quietly hold the breath and count 120 heartbeats while exhaling gently out the mouth. The inhalation and exhalation should be very delicate so that you cannot hear the passing of the breath, and so that a goose feather could be laid over the nostrils and it would not flutter. Through constant practice, gradually increase the count to 1,000 heartbeats. This is the way that the old can daily regain their youth.

Only gradually, over time, did the breathing techniques change their focus from restoring the Three Treasures and stopping the breath to directing the qi to various locations in the body. The seven bamboo tablets of the cloudy satchel (a classic Taoist text indigenous to the Hygiene School of Mt. Hua Shan) provides many examples of this earlier practice, such as in the following excerpt:

> In a supine position, inhale through the nose and stop the breath. If seeking to cure abdominal pains, use intention to direct the qi and, with your imagination, lead it down to the location of the pain. When this location becomes warm, it will then be cured.

Before the process of the Lesser Heavenly Circuit was developed, respiration exercises focused primarily on sending qi to one of the three tan t'ien cavities—the lower, middle, or upper cavity. This practice was similar to kundalini yoga, except that only three qi cavities were focused on rather than seven chakras. As these cavities opened, the qi would be sufficiently stimulated to flow into all the other meridians and collaterals. The focus of this practice soon changed, however, to the orbital movement of the qi around the Function and Control meridians.

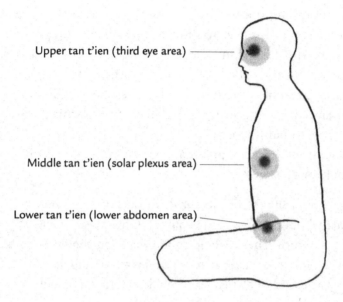

Upper tan t'ien (third eye area) ————

Middle tan t'ien (solar plexus area) ————

Lower tan t'ien (lower abdomen area) ——

The three tan t'ien cavities

The circulation of qi up the spine and down the front of the body (the Lesser Heavenly Circuit) most likely developed from the early Taoist practice of the "returning essence to replenish the brain" method—which is the process of sending restored ching (refined blood and sexual essence) up the spine into the brain.

Keep in mind, however, that the present process of circulating qi through the Lesser Heavenly Circuit was never the starting point for qi circulation that we see in many of the popular Taoist books of today. The idea of circulating qi always existed in Taoism—as a result of the work of regulation (t'iao). But it was not limited to the circulation of qi just through the Function and Control channels; rather, the belief was that qi would circulate through all the meridians and collaterals in the body. Taoists always held that the effects of body regulation (t'iao shen), breath regulation (t'iao hsi), and mind regulation (t'iao hsin) were the catalysts for this type of circulation, which they referred to as mobilizing breath (yun qi) or simply free circulation.

The very purpose of the Eight Brocades—and of this entire book, for that matter—is to help you accomplish what is called circulating qi through the Lesser Heavenly Circuit; which means bringing your qi, or energy, up your back and down the front of your body. However, you must understand that this circulation is in one sense the goal, not necessarily the method.

Using the analogy of a crimped garden hose, uncrimping the hose nearest the spigot is necessary in order to get sufficient water flow and force to open the hose and effect free flow. Qi flow works in the same way: we must free up the qi nearest the lower abdomen in order to get it to flow freely. Too many books and teachers propagate the idea that, if we just imagine the qi circulating, it magically will. Too many people fail with this method, never acquiring qi and ending up quitting. It may, after years and years of practice, produce results, but the most efficient and traditional manner in learning to mobilize qi is first to open up the qi cavities (the crimps) along the qi meridian paths so the qi can flow freely.

This is how Master Liang first taught me to circulate qi—not by just imagining qi circulating. So don't think so much about where you are going; rather, put more attention on how to get there. For without the right method (vehicle) the journey will be in vain.

THE
FIRST
REGIME

EXTERNALLY PATTING

THE EIGHT SUBTLE MERIDIANS

AND TWELVE CAVITIES

Patting is an ancient method of the arts of nourishing life massage; it is usually referred to as kneading or shampooing the muscles. Practices such as pressing the skin, pushing and grasping, and relaxing the bones have developed from this art. The practice of kneading can also include the use of wooden pestles, bean and pebble sacks, and even iron rods (primarily in the martial art world).

The Eight Subtle Qi Meridians are not meridians normally associated with acupuncture. In fact, only two of these meridians—the Control meridian and Function meridian—have associated acupuncture points along their paths. These Eight Subtle Meridians are the channels in which the ching is accumulated and mobilized.

Acupuncture meridians are associated with the flow and accumulation of qi. When the Eight Subtle Meridians are obstructed, neither ching nor qi can move through the channels and collaterals properly, so the stimulation of these subtle meridians is crucial to the adept.

Wooden pestles

Normally, the entire meridian is massaged, but in most cases it is only necessary to pat just around the areas of the Twelve Cavities associated with the meridians, such as the Returning Yin cavity, the Gates of Life cavity, and so forth. On the following pages, you'll find diagrams showing the paths of these meridians, along with a diagram of the Twelve Cavities. Each area requires a somewhat different approach to patting, and the different approaches are given with the descriptions of the meridians and cavities. The correct procedure is to pat the cavities and massage the pathways of the meridians.

Whereas the exercises of the Eight Brocades indeed stimulate these Eight Subtle Meridians, the aim here is to help further the process through external stimulation, especially in the important Function and Control meridians.

The whole subject of kneading is extensive. From ancient times, the Chinese have made use of numerous methods of kneading for curing disease and illness, as well as for nourishing their qi. It is without question an entire science within the self-healing methods of the arts of nourishing life and is well worth investigation. The methods described here are purely those of simple patting and rubbing. And it is vital that you refrain from patting and rubbing too strenuously; keep the stimulation vigorous and use some pressure, but do not work too deeply.

Although I've provided the diagrams showing the pathways of the Eight Subtle Meridians, I have included instructions only on how to massage the Twelve Cavities of the meridians, since in most cases it is necessary only to pat just around these main cavities, and the instructions for rubbing and patting these cavities should be more than sufficient for stimulating and accumulating ching and qi. The diagrams follow this brief introduction and the techniques for massaging the Twelve Cavities are subsequently presented.

The reason these meridians are called subtle is that they are not in effect qi meridians as you would find in acupuncture, with the exceptions of the

Function and Control meridians, which are both ching and qi meridians—and this is the reason they predominate in the practice of inner self-cultivation. Hence, the intention of the first two regimes in *externally patting* and *internally opening* the cavities is precisely to stimulate blood flow in these routes and areas so that ching will accumulate. This in turn strengthens the qi so that it, too, can accumulate in these routes and areas. But too often authors erroneously encourage their readers to simply visualize the qi circulating through these pathways, which only ends in vain.

To truly experience qi circulation in these meridians, one cannot overlook the following basic requirements: increased blood circulation for the accumulation of ching; regulated breath control for the accumulation of qi; a focused intent to bring about the spirit.

The Eight Diagram images associated with the Eight Subtle Meridians correspond to the Fu Hsi arrangement, which is representative of the external realms and corresponds with the external practice of stimulationg these pathways and centers.

The Eight Subtle Meridians

CONTROL MERIDIAN (TU MO)

This meridian begins at the Tailbone cavity and ascends up the spine, continues over the top of the head, and ends on the gum below the nose. This meridian is represented by Heaven (Ch'ien).

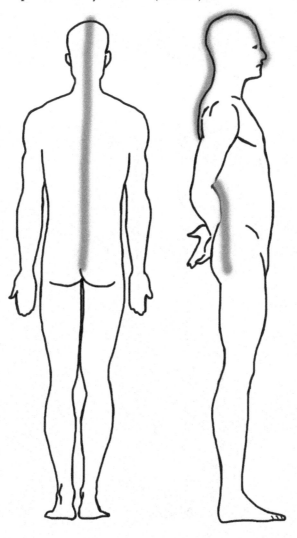

FUNCTION MERIDIAN (JEN MO)

This meridian begins at the Returning Yin cavity, travels directly up the center of the front of the body, and ends just below the lower lip. This meridian is represented by Earth (K'un).

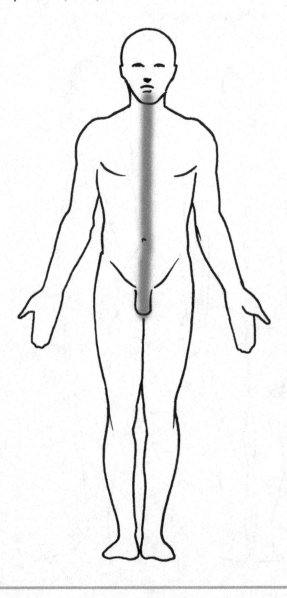

BELT MERIDIAN (TAI MO)

This meridian begins and ends at the Ocean of Qi cavity, traveling completely around the waist. This meridian is represented by fire (li).

Thrusting Meridian (ch'uang mo)

This meridian begins at the Returning Yin cavity, travels up through the genital region, and then rises directly between the Control meridian and Function meridian paths, ending at the heart organ. This meridian is represented by water (k'an).

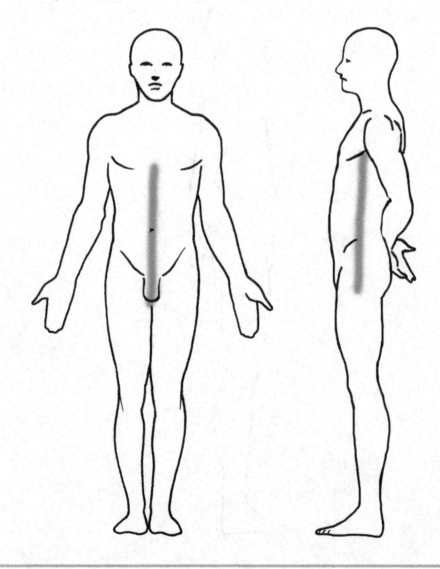

YANG ARM MERIDIAN (YANG WEI MO)

This meridian begins in the Ocean of Qi cavity, moves upward and across both the right and left sides of the chest, into the inner portion of both arms, down into the Dragon and Tiger cavities, and to the tips of the middle fingers. This meridian is represented by valley (tui).

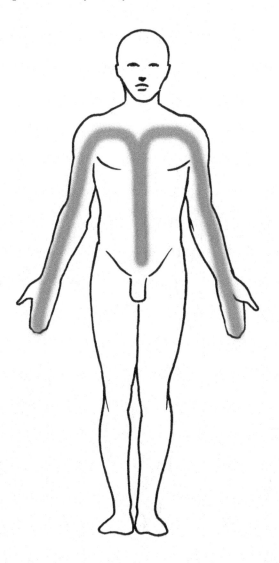

YIN ARM MERIDIAN (YIN WEI MO)

This meridian travels up from the Gates of Life cavity, across both sides of the upper back, through the scapula, into the front area of the arms, and down to the tips of the little fingers. This meridian is represented by wind (sun).

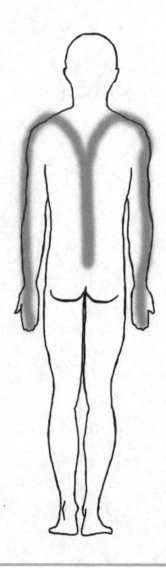

YANG LEG MERIDIAN (YANG CHIAO MO)

This meridian begins on the bottom of the left and right heels, turns outward at the ankles and travels up the outside of the legs and along the left and right sides of the body, up through and meeting at the Mysterious Pass cavity, separating again and traveling over the left and right sides of the head into the Jade Pillow cavity. This meridian is represented by mountain (ken).

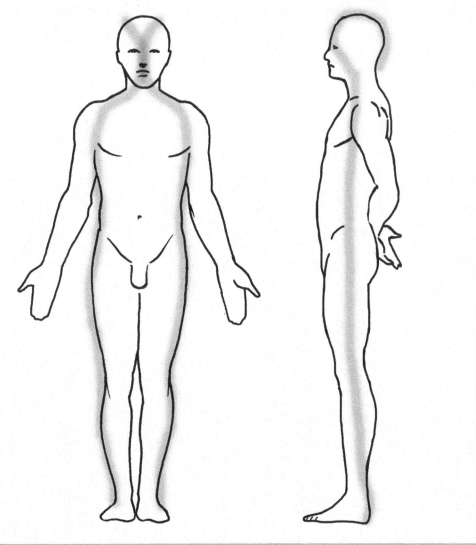

Yin Leg Meridian (Yin chiao mo)

This meridian begins at the insteps of both feet, travels up the inner part of the legs, meets in the Returning Yin cavity region, and proceeds directly up the center of the body into the Mysterious Pass cavity. This meridian is represented by thunder (chen).

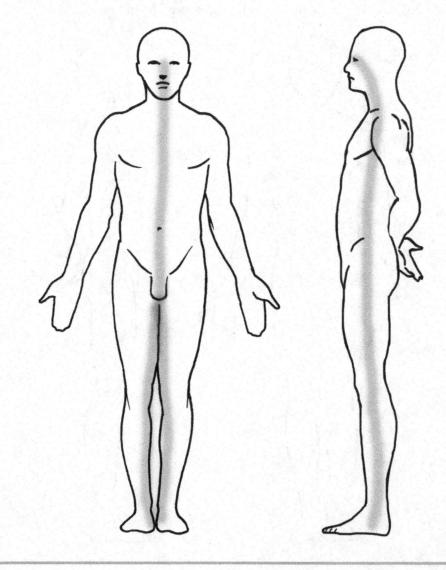

The Twelve Cavities: Methods for Self-Massage

When performing these methods, always start with the left (yang) hand. When the instructions say to rub or pat with the fingers, this means to use the pads of the fingers. Other than when rubbing and patting the small area between the eyebrows (the Mysterious Pass cavity) use all four fingers to circle and pat around each cavity, visualized as an area approximately three inches in diameter.

Rubbing is done in two ways: first, using the left hand (finger pads, sides of the fingers, palms, or fists, depending on the cavity) and then following with the right hand, or second, rubbing with both hands at the same time. When rubbing with the left hand, circle in one direction around the cavity thirty-six times, and *grasp the right hand firmly,* making the Tiger fist, so that you close off the meridian and generate more heat. Then switch positions and circle the right hand around the cavity in the opposite direction thirty-six times and make the Dragon fist with the left hand.

Patting can be done first with the left-hand fingers (finger pads, sides of the fingers, or palms, depending on the cavity) and then with the right-hand fingers, or in an alternating fashion—once with the left hand and then immediately following with the right, then with the left again, and so on.

When directed to heat a cavity, hold the breath and rub the palms together (or, for the Mysterious Pass cavity, rub the index and middle fingers of the left hand into the middle of the right palm in order to heat the fingertips), cover the cavity area with the left hand (palm or fingers, depending on the instructions), place the right hand on the lower abdomen, and perform nine natural breaths.

Although individual instructions will vary, the above information contains the basic ideas for massaging, patting, and heating the Twelve Cavities.

Returning Yin (hui yin): this cavity is located in the perineum area, the soft fleshy area between the anus and penis/vagina base.

- Using the fingers, rub the Returning Yin cavity thirty-six times with the left hand, then thirty-six times with the right.
- Using the fingers of both hands, alternately pat the inner thighs and area of the Returning Yin cavity forty-eight times.

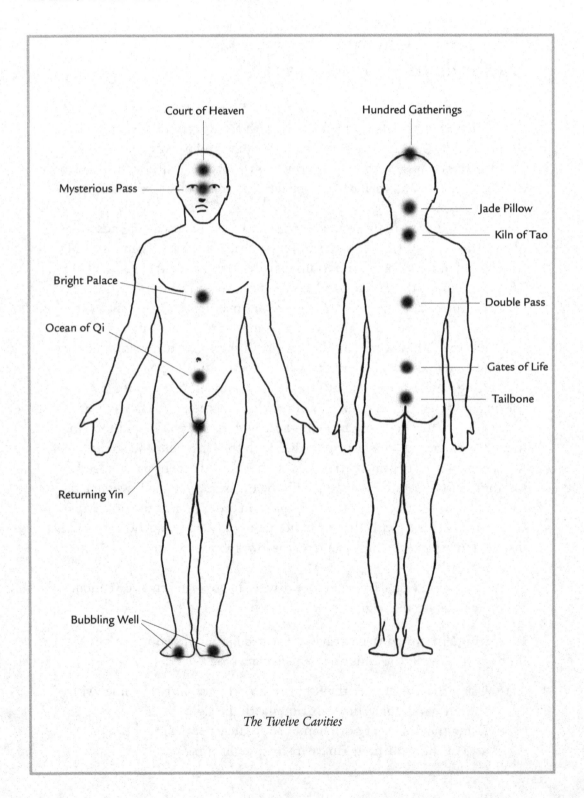

Court of Heaven

Hundred Gatherings

Mysterious Pass

Jade Pillow

Kiln of Tao

Bright Palace

Double Pass

Ocean of Qi

Gates of Life

Tailbone

Returning Yin

Bubbling Well

The Twelve Cavities

Tailbone (wei lu): rub the area of the tailbone and upper buttocks; pat the tip of the tailbone.

- Using the palm sides of the thumb and index fingers of both hands, simultaneously rub the tailbone and upper buttocks thirty-six times.
- Using the fingers, pat the tailbone twenty-four times with the left hand, then twenty-four times with the right.

Gates of Life (ching men): rub the hollow spaces of the lower back, the concave areas located to the sides of the spine; pat the cavity located at the dip of the curve of the spine, directly opposite of the navel.

- Using the back of each fist, simultaneously rub around the Gates of Life cavity thirty-six times.
- Using the sides of the index fingers, alternately pat the Gates of Life cavity forty-eight times.

Double Pass (shuang kuan): this cavity is located in the middle of the back directly over the protruding vertebrae.

- Bringing each arm over the shoulder and using the fingers, pat the Double Pass cavity twenty-four times with the left hand, then twenty-four times with the right.
- If this proves too difficult, draw in the shoulders forty-eight times, pulling them forward and then releasing the pressure.

Kiln of Tao (t'ao tao): rub the entire neck and pat the area covering the base of the neck and the first three vertebrae. (The kiln of Tao cavity is located right on the vertebra that protrudes at the base of the neck.)

- Using the fingers, rub the Kiln of Tao thirty-six times with the left hand, then thirty-six times with the right.
- Using the fingers of both hands, alternately pat the Kiln of Tao forty-eight times.

Jade Pillow (yu chen): rub and pat the areas of the upper neck and the Heavenly Drum, the hollow space where the neck attaches to the skull.

- Using the fingers, rub the Jade Pillow cavity thirty-six times with the left hand, then thirty-six times with the right.
- Using the fingers of both hands, alternately pat the Jade Pillow cavity forty-eight times.

153

Hundred Gatherings (pai hui): this cavity is located on top of the head in the area of the soft spot we had as babies.

- Using the fingers, rub the Hundred Gatherings cavity thirty-six times with the left hand, then thirty-six times with the right. Using the fingers of both hands, alternately pat the Hundred Gatherings cavity forty-eight times. Stop the breath and rub the palms of both hands until they are hot. Then heat the Hundred Gatherings cavity with the left palm, and the lower abdomen with the right palm.
- Breathe nine times.

Court of Heaven (t'ien ting): this cavity is located at the top of the forehead.

- Using the fingers, rub the Court of Heaven thirty-six times with the left hand, then thirty-six times with the right.
- Using the fingers of both hands, alternately pat the Court of Heaven forty-eight times.
- Using the palms, heat the Court of Heaven and the lower abdomen—left hand on the Court of Heaven, right hand on the lower abdomen.
- Breathe nine times.

Mysterious Pass (hsuan kuan): this cavity is located between the eyebrows where the nose attaches to the skull.

- Using the fingers of both hands, simultaneously rub from the Mysterious Pass cavity out to the temples and back thirty-six times.
- Rub the Mysterious Pass cavity thirty-six times with just the left-hand index and middle fingers, then thirty-six times with the right-hand index and middle fingers.
- Using the fingers of both hands, alternately pat the Mysterious Pass cavity forty-eight times.
- Heat the Mysterious Pass cavity and the lower abdomen. First, rub the index and middle fingers of the left hand into the Tiger cavity (middle of the palm) of the right hand. When the fingers and palm are hot, place the two fingers of the left hand onto the Mysterious Pass cavity and the palm of the right hand on the lower abdomen.
- Breathe nine times.

Bright Palace (chiang kung): this cavity is located in the solar plexus region at the base of the sternum.

- Using the palms, rub the Bright Palace cavity thirty-six times with the left hand, then thirty-six times with the right.
- Using the fingers of both hands, alternately pat the Bright Palace cavity forty-eight times.

Ocean of Qi (qi hai): rub and pat the area from the pubic bone to the navel.

- Using the palms of both hands, alternately pat the Ocean of Qi cavity forty-eight times.
- Using the palms, place the left hand on the Ocean of Chi cavity, with the right hand placed on top, and rub seventy-two times, first to the left (counterclockwise) thirty-six times, and then to the right (clockwise) thirty-six times.
- Using the palms of both hands, heat the Ocean of Chi cavity—left hand on the bottom, right hand on top.
- Breathe nine times.

Tiger's Mouth (hu k'o): this cavity is located in the area between the bones of the thumb and index finger.

- Using the left-hand thumb, rub the Tiger's Mouth cavity of the right hand thirty-six times. Then, using the right-hand thumb, rub the Tiger's Mouth cavity of the left hand thirty-six times.
- Using the left-hand thumb, rub the Tiger cavity of the right-hand palm thirty-six times. Then, using the right-hand thumb, rub the Dragon cavity of the left-hand palm thirty-six times. These cavities are located directly in the middle of each palm.
- Rub the finger pads of both middle fingers together forty-eight times.

Bubbling Well (yung ch'uan): rub from the the central area of the bottom of each foot to the center of the balls of the feet.

- Using the thumbs of both hands, simultaneously rub the respective Bubbling Well cavities of each foot thirty-six times.
- Using the right-hand fingers, pat the bottom of the entire left foot, including the instep and heel area, forty-eight times. Then, using the left-hand fingers, pat the same area on the right foot forty-eight times.
- Using the palms of both hands, heat the Bubbling Well cavity of the left foot: place the right palm on the bottom of the foot and the left palm on top of the foot, so the palms are directly opposite each other. The two hands cradle the foot.
- Breathe nine times.
- Heat the Bubbling Well cavity of the right foot, placing the left palm on the bottom of the foot and the right palm on top of the foot.
- Breathe nine times.
- Conclude with the Restoring Youthfulness practice: hold the breath while you rub the hands together to heat them; then cup them over the face, fingertips touching the eyebrows. Breathe nine times. Heat the hands again and lightly rub the face thirty-six times.

THE SECOND REGIME

INTERNALLY OPENING

THE EIGHT SUBTLE QI CAVITIES

This method of the Eight Brocades is directed solely at *internally* opening the main energy centers along the path of the Function and Control meridians. In contrast to the idea of externally patting the meridians, which is similar to pinching and pressing toothpaste from a tube, the internal process can be likened to unblocking a garden hose that has been crimped in eight critical places so that the flow of water is obstructed. If you uncrimp the hose in the area closest to the spigot, and open three or more crimps, the water will have enough force to push through and open the other crimped areas. This is also true of the qi: if you focus initially on the Returning Yin, Gates of Life, Double Pass, and Jade Pillow cavities, the qi can arch up and over through the Hundred Gatherings, Mysterious Pass, and Bright Palace cavities, and then into the Ocean of Qi cavity. Once the cavities along the meridians are opened, the qi will flow of its own accord.

When these cavities are opened, several initial physical reactions can occur. The intensity of the sensations will depend greatly on how obstructed the cavities were to begin with, along with the depth and consistency of practice.

Generally speaking, the physical reactions fall into seven categories: pulsing, heat, tingling, itching, perspiration, surging, and visual occurrences.

1. **Pulsing** is a good reaction, because it means that not only is blood being accumulated in the cavity area but that qi is also.

2. The reaction of **heat** means that not only is there an increase in the blood supply being directed to the cavity area but also that qi is likewise present.

3. **Tingling** is a good sign of increased blood circulation and the initial attraction of qi.

4. The feeling of **itching** is a temporary one, not unlike the reaction from a mosquito bite. The reason the area of a mosquito bite itches is that all the blood has been removed from that area. The itching is meant to restore the blood to the area. When performing this practice, you may draw more blood to an area, but insufficient circulation causes it to dissipate again; thus the area is left dry of blood and an itching sensation results.

5. **Sweating** is a good sign of increased blood circulation, and it aids in the removal of body toxins. However, if not enough qi is present, the qi will not penetrate into the bones. It is always advisable to wear a long-sleeve shirt and pants during practice so that the heat generated from practicing is not dissipated. Do not remove the shirt or pants or take a shower until the sweat has dried. This precaution will help the qi penetrate into the sinews and bones. Sweating is an external expression of qi dissipating. But when the sinews and bones sense heat, this is an expression of penetrating qi, which is much more desirable.

   My t'ai chi ch'uan teacher, Master Tsung-tsai Liang, always practiced with a sweatshirt on. In fact, he wore one almost all the time, even in the heat of summer. He advised students to wear long-sleeve shirts especially when practicing t'ai chi ch'uan, qigong, or meditation, in order to avoid dissipating the generated heat. Likewise, he advised never to shower immediately afterward, rather to wait until the sweat dried naturally.

6. **Surging** is a very good reaction because it means the qi is beginning to actually move (like water surging through the hose when it is uncrimped). This usually creates an involuntary reflex action or an incredible wavelike sensation in the body. But this is still an unconscious response of the qi and is therefore not a controlled action, which is much more preferable.

7. The **visual occurrences** are a difficult subject to discuss because they can take on so many forms, and one needs to clearly distinguish between a real experience and one induced by fanaticism. Positive visions are usually associated with white or clear light and sensations of lightness, and negative ones with darkness and sensations of heaviness.

    One example of a positive vision is seeing raindrops or bubbles floating around you; a negative vision would be dark images darting about your peripheral vision, accompanied by a sense of sluggishness. The subject of positive and negative qi experiences runs an extensive gamut: from feeling content, a positive qi, to being angry, obviously a negative qi, all the way to experiences of visiting heavenly realms (positive qi) to visitations by demons and inhabitants of hell (negative qi).

The method of opening these cavities is to focus all your attention on one of these cavities at a time. Feel and sense your breath expanding and contracting the area with each inhale and exhale. Visualizing each area as a three-inch sphere of white light is best. Start with the Returning Yin cavity, breathe nine, eighteen, thirty-six, or one hundred and eight times, as time permits, and then move up to the next cavity, the Gates of Life, and breathe nine times or more there. Continue in this manner until coming full circle to the Ocean of Qi cavity. If time permits, repeat the whole process three or nine complete times, so that the Lesser Heavenly Circuit is performed.

Some texts recommend a different approach from this one, which is the Lesser Heavenly Circuit. They advise to perform first the Lesser Earthly Circuit, which focuses on the Returning Yin, Gates of Life, and Ocean of Qi cavities only, and to do so until some result of qi is achieved. Afterward, you advance to the Lesser Human Circuit, which includes the Returning Yin,

Gates of Life, Double Pass, Bright Palace, and Ocean of Qi cavities. When results are achieved with this circuit, you can then advance to the Lesser Heavenly Circuit, which includes all eight cavities.

This simpler approach, called the Three Powers—heaven, earth, and man—was also recommended to me by my teacher. He so advised because he thought, as do other authorities, that it allows the practitioner to keep the qi low in the abdomen at first, then gradually advance it higher. Going too fast with these things, as well as allowing the qi to rise too quickly into the upper body and head, is not recommended unless a competent teacher can be with you at all times during the training.

The focused breathing exercise outlined above can be used as a method of meditation after performing the Fourth Brocade, or as an exercise all on its own. The following is a detailed list and explanation of the Eight Subtle Qi Cavities.

The Eight Diagram images shown with each cavity correspond to King Wen's arrangement, which is representative of the internal realms.

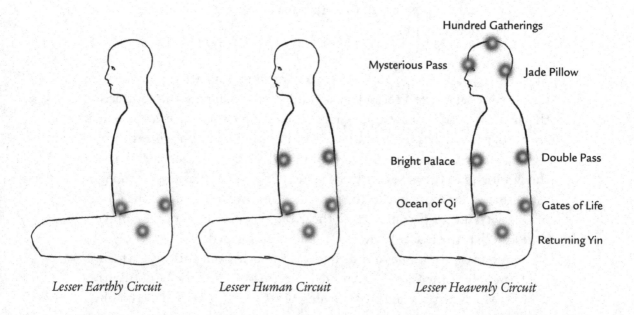

Lesser Earthly Circuit　　　*Lesser Human Circuit*　　　*Lesser Heavenly Circuit*

The Eight Subtle Qi Cavities

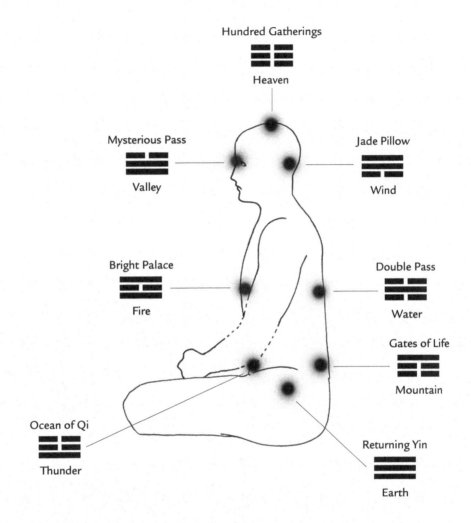

1. Returning Yin cavity (hui yin ch'iao): This cavity, also referred to as the Mortal Gate cavity (sheng szu ch'iao) and sometimes as the Middle Gate cavity (chung men ch'iao), is located in the perineum area, the soft fleshy space between the anus and penis/vagina base. This area is usually very obstructed because of all the tension applied to it, and therefore blood circulation becomes difficult. The postures of both meditation and most qigong practices within the martial arts assure that this area remains open by avoiding positions in which the buttocks would be pinched together. Especially beneficial is the lotus posture of meditation, which opens the area widely and thus releases any obstructions. When this cavity fully opens, you can have the experience of a loud inner bang, like an explosion, along with the sense of an incredibly bad smell. The mind will become full of light, but you will sense a thick, mudlike blackness below. This is similar to a glass of water in which the debris has settled on the bottom while the water above is clear.

This area is symbolized by Earth (K'un).

2. Gates of Life cavity (ching men ch'iao): This cavity is located on the lower back (sacrum). Gates of Life is also used to refer to the kidney organs. This cavity and the kidneys are related in that the Gates of Life are the storehouse of ching (sexual energy). This cavity extends from the tailbone up to the lower middle back. It is very difficult for blood and qi to flow here. Taoists observed that, in babies, this area remains bluish in color for at least the first few days of life. After a few days more blood does reach the area and the skin color becomes normal, but as we age most of us tend to hold a great deal of tension in this area, which exacerbates the natural tendency to a restricted flow of blood. It is precisely restriction in this area that hampers a person's agility. The aim, of course, is to circulate the qi throughout this area. You will perspire greatly here before the cavity opens and will experience a heightened sense of having a very strong spine. Tingling sensations may also be present.

This area is symbolized by mountain (ken).

3. Double Pass cavity (shuang kuan ch'iao): This cavity is both a qi point and an intersection of two qi channels. In early Taoism, this area was referred to as the juncture of the Blue Dragon and White Tiger qi meridians. These two meridians intertwine along the spine and actually pass through each other at this point; hence the name Double Pass. The Double Pass cavity is located in the middle of the back, directly over the protruding vertebrae. Again, it is difficult for qi to pass through this area because the skin and bone are so close together that large quantities of blood cannot gather—as it can, for example, in the hands. This cavity, when opening, renders a sensation of expansion, as though the middle back and shoulder blades actually extend and round the back, like a turtle's. A baby's back is naturally rounded like this. As we grow older, the scapula begin pinching this area, thus obstructing blood and qi.

This area is symbolized by water (k'an). ▦

4. Jade Pillow cavity (yu chen ch'iao): Also called the Heavenly Drum, it is the area of the occiput, where the skull ends and the soft fleshy area of the neck begins. This is another place where the blood and qi can be obstructed, also because the skin and bone are so close. When you are concentrating on this cavity, the eyes must be imagined to have rolled back as if to gaze at the cavity internally. It is imperative that this cavity be pierced, otherwise the qi cannot arch over the top of the head and down into the front of the body. Piercing is literal in that there is an almost lightninglike experience when this cavity opens, or you may hear what sounds like distant voices carried on the wind or drumlike noises. You may also experience severe headache, but all this passes. A redness can also appear directly above this cavity on the skull.

This area is symbolized by wind (sun). ▦

5. Hundred Gatherings cavity (pai hui ch'iao): Also referred to as K'un-lun Shan or "mud ball" (ni wan). This cavity is directly to the front of the area that, on a baby, is called the soft spot. Depending on the amount of blood and qi you can attract to this cavity, some of the softness can be regained. As in the previous procedure, the eyes must be imagined to roll back and gaze upward at this cavity. A good sign this cavity is opening is the experience of seeing what appear to be hundreds of lamps or small lights throughout the inner cranial area, which is accompanied by a profound sense of tranquil joy. This is evidence that the shen has been stimulated internally and that there is qi in the lower abdomen. Lesser signs are the feeling of ants (or itching) on top of the head; heat and pulsing are good signs, but one needs to progress further in order to raise the shen. The shen will rise upward along the spine into the Hundred Gatherings cavity when the ching and qi have congealed in the lower abdomen.

This area is symbolized by Heaven (Ch'ien). ▦

6. Mysterious Pass cavity (hsuan kuan ch'iao): Also called Heavenly Eye (t'ien mu), Hall of Seals (yin t'ang), and Cavity of Origins (tsu ch'iao). More commonly, this is referred to as the third eye or upper tan t'ien (shang tan t'ien). This cavity is located between the eyes and back in one inch. You must direct the gaze of your eyes inward when focusing on this cavity. When the cavity is beginning to open, there will at first be a tingling sensation and then a pulsing reaction in the area.

This area is symbolized by valley (tui).

7. Bright Palace (or Scarlet Palace) cavity (chiang kung ch'iao): Also called the middle tan t'ien (chung tan t'ien). It is located in the solar plexus region at the base of the sternum. The heat generated in this area must be sunk into the lower abdomen in order to get the breath fully into this area. Heat and perspiration are common sensations when this cavity is being opened; a redness can also appear on the chest area directly above it. The chest must be hollowed naturally for the qi to pass through this cavity. The hands and feet will then become consistently warm, and the qi can be directed to them to produce intense heat. Practicing the ingesting of saliva and breath will greatly aid in sinking the qi to the next cavity.

This area is symbolized by fire (li).

8. Ocean of Qi cavity (qi hai ch'iao): Also called the lower tan t'ien (hsia tan t'ien), it is located about three inches below the navel and one inch back into the body. This area is in the pit of the stomach, where there is nothing but emptiness. It is this emptiness that must be filled with qi so that the qi can be adequately transported throughout the body and raise the spirit to the top of the head. The first signs of this cavity beginning to open are vibration felt in the lower abdomen, a feeling of inner warmth, and the breath being really full and natural, noticeably distinct from the normal sense of breathing. The whole body seems to participate in the inhalation and exhalation, not just the lungs or diaphragm. A baby breathes in much the same manner. This is called true breath. Later on, you should sense a thunderous sort of reaction in the lower abdomen. From here, work begins on the method of the Nine Revolutions and the depositing of a drop of pure spirit (yang shen) into the lower abdomen.

This area is symbolized by thunder (chen).

THE
THIRD
REGIME

THE LESSER HEAVENLY CIRCUIT

First lie down on your back in a quiet place with lots of fresh air. Begin filling the body with air through the nose and expelling it out the mouth with a *ha* sound. Perform this nine times. Next, close the mouth and place the tongue on the roof of the mouth and begin breathing naturally, for a total of twenty-four breaths. Then fold the hands over the Bright Palace cavity, with the left hand over the right, and begin holding the breath for twelve heartbeats. This is called the *small cycle*. To advance, perform this last step for a *medium cycle* of sixty heartbeats, and then move on to a *large cycle* of one hundred twenty heartbeats. Those who master one thousand heartbeats have entered the gate of immortality.

While the breath is being held, the qi must be guided by intent down to the Ocean of Qi cavity, into the Returning Yin cavity, and then down the legs into the Bubbling Well cavities; then up into the Gates of Life cavity, then the Jade Pillow cavity, then the Hundred Gatherings cavity, then down into the Mysterious Pass cavity, and finally back into the Bright Palace cavity.

While holding the breath, collect the saliva and, before inhaling new air, gulp it down into the lower abdomen. As described previously, this is called embryonic breathing. When the breath can be held for three hundred heartbeats, the ears will not hear, the eyes will not see, and the mind will be without thoughts.

Then sit up on a mat with legs bent and crossed, the left heel pressed in on the Returning Yin cavity. Regulate your mind, body, and breath. Place the right hand upon the left, drawing both close to the belly to cup the navel area. Next, begin tapping the lower teeth against the upper ones as though eating, thirty-six times, to regulate the body and spirit.

Then, Stir the Sea with the Red Dragon thirty-six times. With the eyes closed, direct the eyeballs to follow the Red Dragon's movements, left and right. Place the tongue against the roof of the mouth. Relax the mind and count the heartbeats up to three hundred sixty times. When the mouth is full of Divine Water, rinse it thirty-six times and then proceed to perform the Four Activities: 1) gently draw in the anus to ensure that the qi has easy access into the Function meridian, which will allow its movement down into the Returning Yin cavity and then up along the spine to pierce the Jade Pillow cavity; 2) place the tongue on the roof of the mouth, forming the magpie bridge; this connects the qi from the Mysterious Pass cavity down to the Bright Palace cavity; 3) with the eyes closed, look upward and back as if to gaze at the Hundred Gatherings and Jade Pillow cavities; this will push the qi up along the Control meridian; 4) hold the breath for twelve heartbeats, which will prevent the qi from dissipating.

Next, swallow one-third of the saliva, sensing both the qi and Divine Water moving downward through the Bright Palace cavity and into the Ocean of Qi cavity. Repeat the Four Activities and swallow two more times, so that three circuits of qi are completed through the Function and Control meridians.

Now, relax the body and mind for a few minutes and then proceed to rub the lower abdomen one hundred eighty times, clockwise, with the left palm over the right. When finished, hold the right palm (with the left palm remaining on top of it) over the lower abdomen to keep it warm. Exposing the lower abdomen to cool air will dissipate the heat previously generated. While holding the lower abdomen, visualize the Ocean of Qi cavity for twenty-four heartbeats.

Then rub the Tiger's Mouth cavities of both hands together until hot and proceed to massage the upper inside part of the eye sockets with the backs of the thumbs, fourteen times. Be careful not to forcibly push inward on the eyeballs. This massaging will relieve any fire in the heart region.

Next massage the sides of the nose thirty-six times with the backs of the thumbs. This will bring relief to the lungs. Still using the backs of the thumbs, massage behind the earlobes fourteen times. This will invigorate the spleen.

Massage the face with open, heated palms fourteen times. This will also strengthen the spleen.

Cover the ears with the palms and beat the Heavenly Drum twenty-four times, left and right. Support the Heavens, slowly, nine times. Repeat both of these procedures three times. While supporting the heavens, inhale pure air through the nose when pushing upward and exhale the impure air out the mouth while gently making the sound *ho* to rid the stomach and lungs of any impurities.

Now, cross the arms over the chest and grasp the shoulders with the hands and shake the body nine times; this will help stabilize the nervous system and bones. Then, with the fingertips, massage the Jade Pillow cavity twenty-four times. Move downward and massage the Gates of Life cavity in the same manner one hundred eight times, and then the Bubbling Well cavities of both feet, one hundred eight times. Last, stand up and go for a walk in the fresh air.

Perform these exercises twice a day, once in the early morning and once in the late evening. In one hundred days, the qi can freely circulate; in one year your youthfulness is restored; and in three years you enter the gate of immortality.

APPENDIX

TO

PART 3

SUMMARY OF INSTRUCTIONS

The Lesser Heavenly Circuit

- In a supine position, perform nine cleansing breaths. Breathe air in through the nose and exhale out the mouth while making the sound *ha*.

- Perform twenty-four natural breaths.

- Place both palms, right hand on the bottom, over the Bright Palace cavity and stop the breath for twelve or more heartbeats.

- With the breath held and using intent, guide the qi through the following cavities: starting with the Bright Palace cavity, move down to the Ocean of Qi and then into the Bubbling Well cavities, then up to the Gates of Life, Jade Pillow, and Hundred Gatherings, down to the Mysterious Pass and back to the Bright Palace. At first you will have to imagine the qi moving through these cavities, but after repeated practice, you can start to sense it.

- Before inhaling, gather the saliva, divide it into thirds, and swallow three times with the sound of *ku ku*.

- Seated in a cross-legged position, place the left-hand palm, with the right hand over the left, on the Ocean of Qi cavity and lower abdomen.

- Breathe nine times.

- Tap the teeth thirty-six times.

- Grasp the hands firmly into fists and perform the Third Brocade, the Red Dragon Stirs the Sea, rousing thirty-six times to the left and thirty-six times to the right.

- Before rinsing and swallowing, breathe 360 times. The number of times is optional; consider this breathing as the meditation part of the exercise and breathe as long as you wish—9, 36, 72, 108, 360, or 1,008 times.

- Rinse the saliva for thirty-six cycles.

- Divide the Divine Water into three equal parts, swallowing three times with the sound of *ku ku* and combining with the Four Activities.

- With the left palm over the right, rub the lower abdomen 180 times in a clockwise direction.

- Keeping the hands over the lower abdomen, focus on the Ocean of Qi cavity for twenty-four natural breaths.

- Rub the Tiger's Mouth cavities of both hands together until hot and massage the eye sockets, using the backs of the thumbs, fourteen times.

- Heat the thumbs again and massage the sides of the nose thirty-six times.

- Using the thumbs, heat and massage behind the earlobes fourteen times.

- Heat the palms by rubbing them together and massage the face fourteen times.

- Alternately beat the Heavenly Drum forty-eight times, and then Support the Heavens nine times. During the latter, inhale when pushing upward and then exhale out the mouth while making the sound *ho*. Repeat both exercises two more times (three times total).

- Shake the shoulders nine times.

- Using the fingers of either the left or the right hand, massage the Jade Pillow cavity in a circular motion twenty-four times.

- Massage the Gates of Life 108 times.
- Massage the Bubbling Well cavities of both feet 108 times.
- Stand up and go for a walk.

SUGGESTED READING

Anderson, Poul. *The Method of Holding the Three Pure Ones: A Taoist Manual of Meditation of the Fourth Century A.D.* Curzon Press, 1980.

Berk, William R., ed. *Chinese Healing Arts: Internal Kung-Fu.* Peace Press, 1979.

Blofeld, John. *Taoism: The Road to Immortality.* Shambhala, 1978.

Chang Chung-yuan. *Creativity and Taoism: A Study of Chinese Philosophy, Art, and Poetry.* Harper Torchbooks, 1963.

Cleary, Thomas, trans. *Awakening to the Tao: Lui I-Ming.* Shambhala, 1988.

——. *The Inner Teachings of Taoism: Chang Po-Tuan; Commentary by Liu I-Ming.* Shambhala, 1986.

——. *The Secret of the Golden Flower: The Classic Chinese Book of Life.* Harper-SanFrancisco, 1991.

——. *Vitality Energy Spirit: A Taoist Source Book.* Shambhala, 1991.

Da Liu. *Taoist Health Exercise Book.* Perigee Books, 1974.

Dean, Kenneth. *Taoist Ritual and Popular Cults of South-East China.* Princeton University Press, 1995.

Girardot, N. J. *Myth and Meaning in Early Taoism: The Theme of Chaos (Hun-Tun).* University of California Press, 1983.

Huang, Jane and Michael Wurmbrand, trans. *The Primordial Breath: An Ancient Chinese Way of Prolonging Life Through Breath Control.* Vols. 1 and 2. Original Books, 1987.

Jou, Tsung-hwa. *The Tao of Meditation: The Way to Enlightenment.* T'ai Chi Foundation, 1983.

Kohn, Livia. *Early Chinese Mysticism: Philosophy and Soteriology in the Taoist Tradition.* Princeton University Press, 1992.

Kohn, Livia, ed. *The Taoist Experience: An Anthology.* State University of New York Press, 1993.

Lu K'uan-yu (Charles Luk). *The Secrets of Chinese Meditations.* Samuel Weiser, 1964.

Nan, Huai-chin. *Tao and Longevity: Mind-Body Transformation.* Translated by Wen Kuan Chu. Samuel Weiser, 1984.

Needham, Joseph. *Science and Civilization in China.* Vols. 1–5. Cambridge University Press, 1954–74.

Robinet, Isabelle. *Taoist Meditation: The Mao Shan Tradition of Great Purity.* Translated by Pas and Girardot. State University of New York Press, 1993.

Veith, Ilza, trans. *The Yellow Emperor's Classic of Internal Medicine.* Berkeley: University of California Press, 1949.

Ware, James R., ed. and trans. *Alchemy, Medicine & Religion in the China of a.d. 320: The Nei P'ien of Ko Hung.* Dover Publications, 1981.

Welch, Holmes. *Taoism: The Parting of the Way.* Beacon Press, 1957.

Welch, Holmes, and Anna Seidel, eds. *Facets of Taoism: Essays in Chinese Religion.* Yale University Press, 1979.

Wong, Eva. *Cultivating Stillness: A Taoist Manual for Transforming Body and Mind.* Shambhala, 1992.

Yang Jwing-ming, M.D. *The Eight Pieces of Brocade.* YMMA, 1988.

Yin Shih-tzu. *Tranquil Sitting.* Translated by Hwang Shi-fu and Cheney Crow. Dragon Door Publications, 1995.

ABOUT THE AUTHOR

In 1979 and 1980, as a resident of Ju Lai Ssu monastery at the City of Ten-Thousand Buddhas in Talmage, California, Stuart Alve Olson began learning the Chinese language and studying Buddhist philosophy, taking formal refuge in Buddhism from Ch'an master Hsuan Hua. While there, he learned the Eight Brocades qigong practices from dharma master Chen Yi.

In 1982 the famous t'ai chi ch'uan master Tung-tsai Liang (presently 102 years old) invited Stuart to live and study with him at his home in St. Cloud, Minnesota. Stuart was the only student ever granted this honor. Stuart stayed in Master Liang's home for more than six years, studying both t'ai chi ch'uan and qigong practices, as well as the Chinese language, all under Master Liang's tutelage. Since then Stuart has traveled extensively throughout the United States with Master Liang, assisting him in his teaching. Stuart has also taught in Canada, Hong Kong, and Indonesia and has traveled throughout Asia. In addition, he has studied massage in both Taiwan and Indonesia.

Stuart presently lives in northern California, where he writes about Asia-related subjects and teaches.

If you wish to contact him please send letters in care of the publisher or e-mail him through his Web site at www.phoenixtaoistcenter.com.

INDEX

Information found in footnotes or illustrations is indicated by an "n" or "i" following the page number.

BOOKS OF RELATED INTEREST

T'ai Chi According to the I Ching
Embodying the Principles of the Book of Changes
by Stuart Alve Olson

The Jade Emperor's Mind Seal Classic
The Taoist Guide to Health, Longevity, and Immortality
by Stuart Alve Olson

Shaolin Qi Gong
Energy in Motion
by Shi Xinggui

The Inner Structure of Tai Chi
Mastering the Classic Forms of Tai Chi Chi Kung
by Mantak Chia and Juan Li

The Secret Teachings of the Tao Te Ching
by Mantak Chia and Tao Huang

Iron Shirt Chi Kung
by Mantak Chia

Bone Marrow Nei Kung
Taoist Techniques for Rejuvenating the Blood and Bone
by Mantak Chia

Shoninki: The Secret Teachings of the Ninja
The 17th-Century Manual on the Art of Concealment
by Master Ninja Natori Masazumi
Commentaries by Axel Mazuer

Inner Traditions • Bear & Company
P.O. Box 388
Rochester, VT 05767
1-800-246-8648
www.InnerTraditions.com

Or contact your local bookseller